The Holocaust

Understanding and Remembering

The Holocaust

Understanding and Remembering

Helen Strahinich

—Issues in Focus—

Enslow Publishers, Inc.

44 Fadem Road   PO Box 38
Box 699   Aldershot
Springfield, NJ 07081 Hants GU12 6BP
USA   UK

Library of Congress Cataloging-in-Publication Data

Strahinich, Helen.
    The Holocaust : understanding and remembering / Helen Strahinich
        p. cm. — (Issues in focus)
    Includes bibliographical references and index.
    Summary: Discusses the circumstances leading up to and the brutal
realities of the murder of millions of Jews and others by the Nazis.
    ISBN 0-89490-725-5
    1. Holocaust, Jewish (1939-1945)—Juvenile literature. [1. Holocaust, Jewish
(1939-1945) 2. World War, 1939-1945—Jews.]
    I. Title. II. Series: Issues in focus (Hillside, N.J.)
    D804.34.S87   1996
    940.53'18—dc20   96-1889
                                                                   CIP
                                                                    AC

Printed in the United States of America

10 9 8 7 6 5 4 3 2 1

Photo Credits: Archives of Mechanical Documentation, Warsaw, Poland,
courtesy of the United States Holocaust Memorial Museum, pp. 44, 49; Enslow
Publishers, Inc., p. 13; Hadassah Rosensaft, courtesy of the United States
Holocaust Memorial Museum, pp. 73, 79; Jewish Historical Institute, Warsaw,
Poland, courtesy of the United States Holocaust Memorial Museum, p. 57;
Museum of Denmark's Fight for Freedom, courtesy of the United States
Holocuast Memorial Museum, p. 68; National Archives, Suitland, MD, courtesy
of the United States Holocaust Memorial Museum, pp. 35, 41; National
Archives, Washington, D.C., courtesy of the United States Holocaust Memorial
Museum, pp. 22, 25, 52, 75, 83; Peter Feigl, courtesy of the United States
Holocaust Memorial Museum, p. 65; United States Holocaust Memorial
Museum, p. 9; William O. McWorkman, courtesy of the United States
Holocaust Memorial Museum, p. 15; Yad Vashem, Jerusalem, Israel, courtesy of
the United States Holocaust Memorial Museum, pp. 30, 39; YIVO Institute for
Jewish Research, New York, courtesy of the United States Holocaust Memorial
Museum, p. 28.

Cover Photo: Flint Born

Contents

Acknowledgments

Many people have helped me with this project. I'd like to thank Aaron Kornblum and Alex Rossino from the United States Holocaust Memorial Museum for their efforts. The folks at One Generation After were also supportive, especially their president, Dr. Rosaline Barron. My friends kept me going and gave valuable advice. Special thanks to Lisa Moore, my first reader; to Carol, my sisters, my mother; and to Flint Born for his photograph. Above all, I'm grateful to my husband, John, and daughters, Nicky and Vanessa, for sticking by me through an obsessive year of research and worry.

1

Understanding the Holocaust

The Holocaust has been called the most terrible catastrophe in modern history: a hideous nightmare that came true, a hell on earth, the hidden battlefront of World War II, and the War against the Jews. It has also been called *Shoah*, a Hebrew word, meaning "a whirlwind of destruction."

The Holocaust was the systematic murder of 6 million Jews during World War II. Before the Holocaust, 9 million Jews lived in Europe. They made their homes in about twenty European countries. Some were artists, playwrights, architects, writers, or musicians. Others were wealthy businesspeople, doctors, lawyers, scientists, or engineers. But most European Jews were average people with average incomes. By the end of World War II, two thirds of them were dead.

German scientists, businesspeople, industrialists, and civil servants contributed to the killing effort. In this way, the Nazis created a "machinery" for mass murder. It worked with fast and brutal efficiency.

The Jews, however, were not the only victims of Nazi hatred. The Nazis also murdered 5 to 6 million Gypsies, people with handicaps, Communists, Jehovah's Witnesses, homosexuals, labor unionists, political prisoners, and prisoners of war.

The Jews, however, suffered such staggering losses that a new word was created to describe what happened to them: *genocide.* Genocide means the systematic murder of a whole group of people because of their race, religion, or nationality.

Who was Adolf Hitler?

Adolf Hitler has been called a monster, the devil, the Antichrist, a demonic dictator, a megalomaniac, a spellbinder, and the most evil genius of the twentieth century. He was elected as chancellor of Germany on January 30, 1933. For twelve years, he led his country on a rampage of war, destruction, and death.

A hypnotic speaker, Hitler used fear, hate, lies, and violence to grab and hold attention and power. He understood the value of propaganda, the use of lies and half-truths to get people to go along with certain ideas or attitudes. To build support, Hitler held huge parades and rallies. Nazi party members waved giant swastikas, the Nazi symbol. They raised their right arms in the Nazi salute and chanted *"Heil Hitler"*—"Hail, Hitler."

Hitler's rise to power came during the Great Depression of the 1930s. After being defeated in World War I, the Germans had struggled without success to get back

Adolf Hitler used propaganda, parades, and rallies to gain support.
Here, thirty-five thousand Nazi troops stand in Berlin to celebrate
the third anniversary of Hitler's chancellorship.

on their feet. Their government was divided and weak. By the time of the Depression, millions of Germans were already unemployed. German factories were silent. Millions of hungry people waited in breadlines with buckets of currency that were nearly worthless. At this time, Hitler gave the Germans a scapegoat: mostly, the Jews. Now the Germans had somebody to blame for their troubles.

Who Were the Nazis?

The Nazis were members of Hitler's party, the National Socialist German Workers' Party. The Nazis wanted to rid Germany of all Jews. They dreamed of making Germany a world power. The Nazis also wanted to do away with the Treaty of Versailles.

Germany had signed this treaty in 1919, after its defeat in World War I. It turned over land to France and Poland that many Germans believed was theirs. It forced Germany to take responsibility for starting World War I. It made Germany pay huge fines, called reparations, for starting the war. The treaty also forced Germany to disarm, reducing the size and strength of its armed forces.

Hitler had joined the Nazi party in 1919, when it was still called the German Workers' Party. At that time it was a small, marginal group. Soon, Hitler took charge of party propaganda. He developed his skills as a speaker and organizer.

To keep order at party meetings, Hitler pulled together a group of men known as Brown Shirts because of the color of their uniform. Hitler made them his *Sturmabteilung,* or S.A., the German term for storm troopers. Soon the Brown Shirts were breaking up meetings of Hitler's opponents.

Hitler and his party went through ups and downs over the next ten years. In December 1924, they received less than 1 million votes. Most people believed that Nazism had no future.[1]

By July 31, 1932, however, Hitler's vote was 13.7 million.[2] The Nazi party was Germany's largest party in the Reichstag, the German parliament. Although Hitler did not have a majority, his opposition remained divided. Always a master politician, Hitler took advantage of his opponents' weaknesses, playing them against each other. On January 30, 1933, he was named chancellor of Germany by the aging President Von Hindenberg. Within one year, Hitler was dictator, ruling over others with absolute power—often with brutality and force—and the Nazi party was the only official party permitted in Germany.

What Was the "Final Solution?"

From early on, Hitler spoke and wrote about getting rid of Germany's Jews. At first, the Nazi plan was to force all Jews to immigrate to other countries. At one point, Hitler had hopes of sending the Jews to the island of Madagascar, off southeastern Africa.[3] Then World War II started. By then, the Nazis had control of countries in which several million Jews lived. They couldn't ship them off to Africa in the middle of the war.

So the Nazis decided to kill them all—every Jewish man, woman, and child. On January 20, 1942, Nazi leaders met in the Berlin suburb of Wannsee. At the

11

Wannsee Conference, they worked out the details for mass murder. They discussed what killing methods to use. The Nazis called their plan the "final solution to the Jewish problem."

What Was World War II About?

Long before Hitler became dictator, he promised to make Germany a world power. His plan was to expand the German empire eastward. First, he would move into neighboring areas, where Germans lived. Then he would push into Poland and Russia. Hitler wrote about his plans in his book *Mein Kampf.* (Most people thought these ideas were just nonsense. They did not take them seriously at first.)

Within a few years after Hitler came to power, he began preparing Germany for war. He increased the size of the German army. He built up the German navy and air force. At the same time, German industry geared up for the war effort. The Germans manufactured ammunition, tanks, submarines, fighter planes, bombers, and other materials needed for fighting a war.[4]

Building up the German armed forces violated the Treaty of Versailles. But Hitler had no intention of honoring the treaty. To fool the western powers, he lied—promising one thing, then doing the opposite. He did not want the rest of Europe to unite again for a war against Germany. So he made speeches about his wishes for peace. He declared Germany's willingness to disarm. All the while, he was getting Germany ready to fight another war.

England, France, the United States, and Russia were all tired of war. Like Germany, these countries had all suffered terrible losses in World War I.

12

Because of a desire for peace, the western powers failed to stop Hitler early on. In fact, most of them made agreements and treaties with Germany. They tried to appease, or satisfy, Hitler by giving in to his demands. They let him rearm Germany. They let him carry out the first part of his plan for world domination. They allowed Hitler to do all this without raising a weapon, or even a serious objection.

On March 2, 1936, Germany marched into and occupied the Rhineland, an area about the size of

This map of Eastern/Central Europe in 1936 shows the Rhineland.

13

Maryland in southwestern Germany between the Rhine River and the part of the border that Germany shares with Belgium, France, and the Netherlands. The Treaty of Versailles prohibited Germany from occupying this neutral territory. Nevertheless, none of the western powers took action. They might have easily defeated Hitler at that point. But they were divided and afraid of starting another big war.

Hitler's next target was Austria, the country of his birth. Many Germans lived in Austria. It shares a southern border with Germany. It also has a similar culture. Behind the scenes, Hitler worked out an arrangement with Austrian leaders to make Austria a part of Germany. On March 12, 1938, Nazi troops marched into the country and took it over without firing a single shot.

For the Jews of Austria, this takeover, or *Anschluss,* was a disaster. The Nazis moved quickly to destroy the rights of Austria's Jews. As Eva Edmunds, who was Jewish and eight years old at the time, explained:

> The streets were full of men in uniform, wearing armbands bearing the letters S.A. or S.S. Many people were starting to wear the Swastika on their coat lapels. These were the Aryans. Non-Aryans, I learned, were subjected to all kinds of indignities, like scrubbing the sidewalks, cleaning bathrooms, and the like.
>
> Elegantly dressed women seemed to be singled out for these jobs. If we saw a gathering of people, we quickly crossed the street or turned into a side street. We wore our oldest clothes, and my mother stopped wearing makeup. We wanted to be as inconspicuous as possible.[5]

While making speeches for peace to fool the rest of the world, Hitler was preparing Germany for war. Even children were included in his war efforts. Here, the Hitler youth march before their leader, Baldur von Schirach (saluting), and other Nazi officials.

The *Anschluss* did not satisfy Hitler. With Austria in his pocket, Hitler turned his eyes toward Czechoslovakia. He pretended to be worried about the well-being of German people living there. But this was just an excuse to take over Czechoslovakia's rich resources and important war defenses. Once again, Hitler was able to reach this goal without a battle.

England and France were still intent on keeping the peace. On September 29, 1938, they signed the Munich Agreement with Germany. This agreement gave Germany a part of Czechoslovakia called the Sudetenland. The Sudetenland held coal and iron mines, chemicals, power plants, and factories. It also contained important parts of Czechoslovakia's defense, telephone, telegraph, and railroad systems. With the Munich Agreement, all of this was lost. And it was lost without a fight.

What did England and France get from the Munich Agreement? For the moment, they got to maintain the illusion of peace. After all, Hitler had promised not to make war in return for the Sudetenland. He had also promised to honor Czechoslovakia's independence. Within a short time, however, the Nazis took over the rest of Czechoslovakia.

Hitler, of course, had plans for world power all along. He had been building up the Nazis' war machine for years. With Austria, Czechoslovakia, and the Rhineland in Nazi hands, Hitler was in a strong position. At last the Western powers understood that they could not trust Hitler's promises. Their desperate efforts to satisfy Hitler had only weakened their position.

On September 1, 1939—less than a year after the Munich Agreement—Hitler invaded Poland. This invasion started World War II. England, France, and, in time, Russia and the United States formed what was called the Allied forces to fight the Nazis. Germany joined Italy and Japan in the Axis alliance. World War II, the bloodiest war in all history, became a battle over the future of the world—between dictatorship and freedom.

Fighting a world war did not stop the Nazis from waging their hidden battlefront against the Jews. This secret war cost the Nazis men, energy, and resources. Railroads needed by the German army were often tied up carrying Jews to death camps. Special killing units, attached to the army, were trained to hunt down and murder Jews. As World War II went on and eventually turned against Germany, the Nazis did not, however, relax their assault against the Jews. Determined to exterminate the Jews, the Nazis murdered them in greater and greater numbers.

2

The Road to Destruction

The Nazis used violence to grab power and to keep it. For many years, Nazis terrorized their opponents, breaking up meetings and beating up members of other parties. After coming to power, the Nazis moved quickly to crush the opposition once and for all. Brown Shirts roamed the streets, attacking and murdering citizens. They broke into homes and threw their opponents into jails and concentration camps. To silence any form of protest, Hitler also abolished free speech, free press, and the right to assembly.

Hitler's oppressive measures worked. Few Germans openly criticized the Nazis when their attacks on Jewish citizens grew more deadly. Those who dared to protest risked the same fate as the Jews. Even worse, many Germans were willing to go along with whatever Hitler asked. They longed for the glory days that he promised them. As a result, many Germans joined the Nazi party.

Many, but not all, participated directly and indirectly in the destruction of the Jews.

Germany provided fertile soil for Hitler's violent anti-Semitism. After all, prejudice against the Jews was nothing new in Europe or in Germany. Hitler's ideas and policies grew out of a long history of violence and hatred toward European Jews.

The Roots of Anti-Semitism

Before Hitler's rise to power, the Jews had lived in Europe for over two thousand years. In the early days of Christianity, Christians tried to convert the beliefs of the small Jewish minority. The Christians believed that Christianity was the only true religion. Their goal was to save Jewish souls. For the most part, their efforts failed. The Jews refused to give up their faith.

As a result, Christians took strong measures against the Jews. They burned the Talmud, the collection of writings that makes up the Jewish civil and religious laws, and other Jewish holy books. They prohibited the Jews from setting up temples for worship. In some places, they burned Jews at the stake for practicing their religion. In other places they crowded the Jews into dirty ghettos—quarters of cities where Jews were required to live—expelled them from the country, or wiped out their towns.

From the fourth century to the nineteenth century, church laws limited the rights of Jews. The states of Europe helped to carry out these measures. Jews could not rent or own property outside the ghetto. They could not become lawyers, pharmacists, notaries, painters, or

19

architects. They could not get academic degrees, and they could not hold public office.

Other laws isolated the Jews from Christians. Jewish doctors could not have Christian patients. Jews could not marry Christians, eat with them, or employ them. Jews could not even discuss religion with Christians.[1]

Still other laws made the Jews stand out from the rest of the population. In some places, Jews had to wear special badges or carry special documents. At times, Jews could only have so-called Jewish names, such as Sarah or Isaac, which are taken from the Old Testament.

To justify such harsh treatment, people spread many lies about the Jews. They blamed the Jews for causing plagues and for poisoning wells. They said the Jews were friends of the devil. They accused the Jews of being thieves and of murdering Christian babies. They even accused the Jews of killing Jesus. These lies helped those who hated the Jews to carry out their brutal acts.

The Beginning of the Terror

By the start of the twentieth century, Jews had gained most of the same rights as other citizens in western Europe. In Germany, the Jewish community was small, only six hundred thousand—or 1 percent—of a population of 60 million.[2] Jews lived and worked in all parts of German society. However, many people in Germany and in Europe still believed the old lies about the Jews. Some writers and politicians, including Hitler, were outspoken anti-Semites.

From his youth, Hitler had despised the Jews. To Hitler, Jews were not Germans. To him, they were polluters, spoiling the German race. Hitler's plan was to rid Germany of all Jews.

Boycott

Hitler's first official act against the Jews was a boycott of Jewish businesses and shops starting April 1, 1933. Nazis posted signs on Jewish stores. They painted doors and windows of stores with Stars of David. They passed out leaflets, asking Germans not to buy from Jews. They blocked entrances to Jewish shops. The Nazis held giant rallies to promote their boycott. But some Germans refused to go along. The boycott was cancelled within twenty-four hours.

Within a week after the boycott, the Nazis issued the first of a series of anti-Jewish laws. Many of these measures resembled the old church laws against the Jews. Issued between 1933 and 1939, these measures:

ANTI-JEWISH LAWS

• forced Jews from jobs in the civil service and industry

• barred Jews from many professions

• excluded Jewish young people from schools and universities

• forced Jews to carry special identification cards

• forced Jews to have their passports stamped with a red "J"

• excluded Jews from sleeper cars or dining cars on trains

• outlawed marriages between Christians and Jews

• prohibited Jews from hiring German women under forty-five

• barred Jews from many spas, public baths, and certain park areas[3]

Beginning April 1, 1933, Nazis organized a boycott of Jewish stores. Here, a woman stands outside a store window reading a sign posted during the boycott.

These measures—four hundred in all—wiped out many of the rights and freedoms of Germany's Jews.[4] These laws also isolated Jewish citizens and took away the ability of many Jews to earn a living. Later, the Nazis also forced the Jews to wear in public a yellow Jewish star, like the one on the cover of this book.

Book Burnings

The Nazis called on the German people to "purify" German culture. On the night of May 10, 1933, thousands of students and professors went on a rampage. Waving torches, they paraded in thirty different cities. They dumped thousands of books written by authors that the Nazis did not like into bonfires.

By this time, Dr. Paul Joseph Goebbels, the Nazi propaganda minister, oversaw the publication of all German books and plays. German anthologies no longer included Jewish writers and poets. Only ghetto publishers would publish books by Jewish writers. Non-Jews could not even buy books written by Jews. The Nazis excluded Jews from the other arts as well. They banned the works of Jewish composers. They kicked Jewish musicians out of symphonies. Jewish painters could not exhibit in German galleries.[5]

Even the cultural life of Germany now bore the Nazi stamp of approval. Only "approved art" was accepted by the Nazis.

Kristallnacht : Crystal Night

Kristallnacht means "night of the broken glass." On the night of November 9, 1938, the Nazis attacked the Jewish communities. They destroyed, looted, and

23

burned over one thousand synagogues. They wrecked over seven thousand businesses.[7] They ruined Jewish hospitals, schools, cemeteries, and homes. Anna Bluethe, a Jewish woman, explained what happened in Kaiserslautern, Germany, when the Nazis terrorized her family on *Kristallnacht*:

> The glass doors of the bookcase were the first object of their wrath. All the books were torn off the shelves and either thrown on the floor or through windows into the street. A similar fate awaited all the papers, documents and other matters, which father kept in his writing desk. Having this accomplished they overturned all the furniture including the heavy safe . . . throwing part of the other furniture on top of the safe.[8]

When the pogrom—an organized display of persecution—ended, ninety-six Jews were dead and thirty thousand arrested.[9] For prison space, the Nazis expanded three concentration camps. These were camps with dismal living conditions where the people were confined against their will. The Jews themselves had to clean up the mess. After *Kristallnacht*, life became even more unbearable for the Jews in Nazi Germany, as Anna Bleuthe explained:

> The days that followed saw anti-Jewish laws passed . . . imposed heavy fines on them, instituted the forced sale of their businesses. The cost of repairing the damage, caused by the destruction, to buildings and properties, had to be carried by the respective Jewish family. Any insurance money that could be claimed for the damage had to be handed over to the state.[10]

24

Thousands of Jews committed suicide. Many Jewish families, like Anna Bluethe's, who could escape, did. As it turned out, however, there would be no escape for most of Europe's Jews.

The Ghettos

Most of Europe's 9 million Jews lived in Eastern Europe. Poland alone held 3.3 million Jews, 10 percent of the total population of Poland.[11] As the Nazis took over Eastern Europe, they forced the local Jews from their homes. Then the Nazis moved the Jews into the most

Germans pass by the broken shop window of a Jewish-owned business that was destroyed during *Kristallnacht*.

rundown part of the city. Tens of thousands of people were crowded into small areas called ghettos. In the ghettos, the Jews lived ten or fifteen in a space adequate for two.[12]

Joseph Soski described what happened when the Nazis occupied Kraków, Poland:

> Daily, they posted all over town, new decrees and orders in German and Polish. In the beginning, those were for the whole population without exception, as: to turn in all weapons, radios, photo-cameras, curfews, etc. But soon these decrees and orders were strictly and only for Jews . . . Jews living in more affluent areas were ordered to vacate their homes. Most of the time [they] were given 15–30 minutes and allowed to take with them only what they could carry by hand.[13]

The Nazis forced the Jews of each community to elect a council. These councils, called *Judenrat,* had to do the Nazis' dirty work for them. They organized and carried out the relocation of other Jews to the ghettos.

Using walls, barbed wire, or fences, the Nazis often cut off large ghettos from the rest of the city. They allowed the Jews of the ghettos little food, medicine, or fuel. Sanitation was poor. Lice infested the ghettos. The inhabitants were always hungry. Corpses littered the streets.

William Mishell, who wrote a book about his experiences in the Lithuanian ghetto of Kovno, explained what happened during the cold winter of 1941–1942, when there was no firewood.

> Temperatures of minus 40 degrees Fahrenheit were common for weeks. . . . Eating cold food, washing with cold water, and sleeping in unheated quarters

took a toll on the population. In desperation people looked for a solution to the problem. Our house, like so many others, was neatly surrounded by a wooden fence, and at night we would go out and rip off a plank or two and sneak it into the house. However, we were not the only ones to notice this unexpected good fortune. Suddenly planks all over were disappearing overnight and people started noticing it. One morning, spontaneously, there was a rush to the fences. . . . Thousands of people, men, women, and even children, descended on the fences with picks, hammers, or any tool that was handy and, yelling and screaming, began fighting each other over every plank or piece of wood.[14]

In the Warsaw ghetto in Poland, about 1 percent of the population (or one of every one hundred people) died each month.[15] For the Nazis, however, the Jews were not dying fast enough.

Einsatzgruppen: Mobile Killing Units

On June 22, 1941, the Nazis invaded the Soviet Union. They called their invasion *Barbarossa*. With this invasion, the Nazis intended to carry out their "final solution."

The Nazis set up four mobile killing units, known as *Einsatzgruppen*. A total of about three thousand volunteers were attached to these units.[16] Their purpose was to murder Jews and Communist officials. As the Nazi armed forces moved into the Soviet Union, the *Einsatzgruppen* followed closely behind. Moving with great speed, they often surprised their victims.

Wherever they went, the *Einsatzgruppen* used the same basic procedure. They chose a supposedly secret

27

An *Einsatzgruppen* soldier is about to shoot a Russian Jew as he kneels at the edge of a grave while other soldiers look on.

gravesite out of town. With the help of local collaborators, they collected Jews. The Nazis forced the Jews to turn over all valuables. They made them take off their clothes. Then they shot them. Mishell described an "action," as these assaults on the Jews were called:

> One hundred at a time, people were selected and told that they were going to wash up. They were told to undress and were promised new clothes after the bath. But when they reached the trenches the guards fell upon them, beating and chasing them until they fell over each other and were immediately shot by Lithuanian partisans. The cries from the children and the mothers were deafening, but the murderers calmly proceeded with their work.[17]

In early 1942, the Nazis added gas vans to the *Einsatzgruppen* arsenals. They forced victims into the vans. Then they hosed carbon monoxide inside. Victims died of suffocation.

By the end of 1942, the mobile killing units had finished their work. In all they had murdered about 1.4 million Jews.[18] The Nazis began using another killing method to complete the final solution—the death camps.

Some Jews, like the Bielski group pictured here, realized they were doomed if they stayed in the ghetto. So they escaped to nearby forests to fight with partisans against the Nazis.

RESISTANCE: FOR HONOR AND REVENGE

At first, the Jews tried to accomodate the Nazis. They accepted the Nazi's anti-Jewish laws. They worked to make themselves useful, even essential, to the German war effort. They knew the Nazis would take swift, harsh measures to wipe out any resistance. So the Jews did nothing to antagonize their powerful persecutors. By early 1942, however, the Nazis' true intentions became clear: They planned to annihilate the Jews.

In the ghettos, some young Jewish men and women prepared to fight to the death—for honor and revenge. They got weapons, collected supplies, and built hiding places. But often these resistance groups did not get support from the rest of the ghetto Jews. The others feared that these young people would bring the anger of the Nazis down on everyone.

Only in the Warsaw ghetto did the resistance succeed. When the Nazis came, the ghetto launched a ferocious attack. They threw homemade bombs at the troops. They blew up mines. Soon, the Germans brought in tanks and heavy ammunition. They set up machine guns on rooftops. But none of the ghetto Jews would surrender. The Nazis torched buildings. Most of the ghetto was in flames. Still, the resistance held out for three weeks. When the fighting ended, the Warsaw ghetto had become a giant graveyard.[6]

Rather than join an armed group in the ghetto, some young people tried to escape. They hoped to band up with partisans, hiding in nearby forests. These groups sabotaged the Nazis. They blew up railroad tracks and bridges, cut telephone wires, and ambushed troops.

The life of a partisan was filled with danger and hardship: informers told the Nazis where they were hiding. Food and weapons were scarce. They were always on the move. Sometimes non-Jewish partisans would turn on them. The Nazis often tried to bomb their bases.

Choosing to fight the enemy often meant death. But some of those brave fighters managed to survive and share their stories with the world.

3

The Camps

The Nazis set up their first concentration camp in 1933, six years before the start of World War II. Located ten miles northwest of Munich, Germany, it was called Dachau.[1] The Nazis built this prison camp to hold political prisoners in one place, and thus "concentrate" their population.

The S.A. guards and S.S. guards, members of the private Nazi army, ran the Dachau camp with cruel efficiency. Prisoners were forced to work at backbreaking and often useless jobs. Those who refused to work or disobeyed a guard could be shot or hanged on the spot.[2] The Nazis wanted to destroy the bodies, minds, and spirits of their prisoners.[3]

Dachau became the model for additional large camps: Sachsenhausen (established in 1936), Buchenwald (1937), Flossenburg (1938), Mauthausen (1938), and Ravensbrück (1939).[4] The Nazis built many smaller camps, too. Guards were trained to use the brutal methods developed at Dachau in these new camps. The Nazis did not try to hide their terrible treatment of political prisoners. They wanted to frighten any remaining opponents in Germany.

Karl Ibach was a young man when he joined the Social Workers' Youth League and demonstrated against the Nazis. He was arrested and kept in a concentration camp for three months.

> We were set useless tasks to do, like taking stones out of the freezing water of the River Wupper, and hunting for concealed weapons in the sewers. . . . If they wanted more information out of you, they would lock you in a metal locker and then kick it, turn it upside down, blow cigarette smoke through its ventilation holes—or worse, before they put you in, they'd make you eat a "Kemna-cut," which was salt herring smeared with cup-grease. Those who refused to eat them were beaten bloody. Those who ate them and then vomited were forced to eat their vomit.[5]

The Concentration Camp System during World War II

In 1939, with the start of World War II, the Nazis began to build more concentration camps. As the German army moved into Austria and then Poland, they added camps in those countries. The Nazis filled these new camps with political opponents, prisoners of war, criminals, Jews, and all other "undesirables" from the occupied countries. Anyone who posed a threat to the Nazis, including ministers and priests, might end up in a camp.

By the early 1940s, the Nazis had turned the concentration camps into a huge slave labor empire. Germany badly needed workers for its war effort, and the enlarged camp system provided a huge, free labor pool.[6]

During this time, the Nazis destroyed many of the Jewish ghettos they had set up. They shot or gassed most of the inhabitants. But they saved the healthiest young people for slave labor. Joseph Soski, who worked as a slave laborer, recalled how the Nazis selected who would live and who would die.

> At one of the street corners, stood the Nazi S.S. men and [they] conducted the selection. One by one each Jew had to walk by. Those with working papers were asked a few questions about age and trade, and if it was to their liking, the Jew was told to step aside and wait. All others, men, women, young and old and those with children were ordered to march toward the railroad spur.[7]

In all, the Nazis built twenty-three main camps. Attached to many of the larger camps were smaller camps, or subcamps. Dachau, for example, had 168 subcamps. Buchenwald had 133.[8] In all, there were about one thousand subcamps. Many of these subcamps had factories where inmates worked.[9]

The population of registered inmates swelled from twenty to thirty thousand in the 1930s to one hundred thousand in late 1942, and to over seven hundred thousand in January 1945. A total of 1.5 million prisoners passed through these labor camps. About half of them died.[10]

The Nazis also "rented" inmates to German companies—and kept the money from their wages. Prisoners

Inmates were forced to work at the Mauthausen concentration camp. Concentration camps provided the Nazis with a huge pool of free-labor workers.

slaved in factories, on farms, in mines, in logging camps, and in rock quarries. Many large companies profited from slave labor. Some, such as I. G. Farben, BMW, and Krupps, are still in business today.[11]

The concentration camps were brutal. Guards treated the inmates worse than slaves. They didn't care whether their prisoners lived or died—especially the Jewish inmates. In fact, they viewed the camps as another way to get rid of Jews. Prisoners worked long, hard hours, seven days a week. They were beaten and starved, as their testimony shows:

> We had one meal in the morning after roll call—a piece of old bread, a bit of marmalade, sometimes a piece of cheese crawling with worms, and coffee-colored liquid. We went to work digging trenches in the forest. My feet were freezing. I was beaten, hit twenty-five times, my nose broken, with broken ribs and a lung hemorrhage.[12]

> We were "living" in terrible conditions, sleeping on the floor dressed, squeezed one next to each other like sardines in a can. The sanitary conditions [were] unbearable. The smell from the only toilet, which was overflowing with human waste, and on top of it—lice, they were eating us up. We tried to kill them, but of no avail. There were no washing facilities at all.[13]

The lack of sanitation led to disease. To make matters worse, prisoners had to put up with evil guards who tortured and humiliated them. Nazi doctors carried out phoney, cruel experiments on camp prisoners—often young children.

36

If they told you to do something, you went to do it. There was no yes or no, no choices. I worked in the crematorium for about eleven months. I saw Dr. Mengele's experiments on children. I knew the kids that became vegetables. Later in Buchenwald I saw Ilse Koch with a hose and regulator, trying to get pressure to make a hole in a woman's stomach. I saw them cutting . . . people in pieces. I was in Flossenburg for two weeks, and they shot 25,000 Russian soldiers, and we put them down on wooden logs and burned them. Every day the killing, the hanging, the shooting, the crematorium smell, the ovens, and the smoke going out.[14]

The Killing Camps

In 1941, Hitler decided to carry out his "Final Solution," the murder of all European Jews. Concentration camps provided one way to carry out Hitler's plan—by working Jewish inmates to death. The Nazis called this method "extermination through labor." But it proved to be a very slow way to get rid of the Jews.

The Nazis wanted a quicker "solution." The *Einsatzgruppen* was one answer. These mobile killing units had certain shortcomings, however. The massacres were too bloody, and too public. Also the gas vans broke down in bad weather. Squad members sometimes got headaches from unloading the vans. Civilians watched and sometimes shot pictures. Also, the bloodshed took a toll on the S.S. Many troopers drank heavily, and some had nervous breakdowns.[15]

So the Nazis found another solution, one that was fast, neat, and secret, for a while anyway. They set up death camps in Poland. The first, Chelmno, opened in late 1941. Belzec and Sobibor opened in 1942. Majdanek and Treblinka, two labor camps, were turned into death camps that same year. The only purpose of the Nazi death camps was mass murder—mostly of Jews and Gypsies. Inside these camps, the Nazis set up gas chambers that killed thousands of people each day.[16]

The Nazis chose Poland as the site of their death camps for a few reasons. Many Jews were concentrated in nearby ghettos. Also, Poland had a good railroad system. Thus, the Nazis could quickly and efficiently transport their victims from the ghettos to the camps.

The Nazis built these killing centers in remote areas in order to hide what they were doing. To keep their secret and fool their victims, the Nazis lied. The Nazis didn't want their prisoners to put up a fight. After all, resistance would make the job harder for the S.S. guards.

THE CHILDREN

The Nazis did not spare the children. Two million children died of cold, heat, starvation, thirst, beating, crushing, piercing, disease, abuse, fire, gunshot, and gassing.[17] At the final count, almost nine out of ten Jewish children who were alive before World War II died during the Holocaust.[18]

So the Nazis told their victims that they were going to labor camps. Sometimes they offered bread and jam to anyone signing up for a transport from the ghetto to these "labor camps." To keep up the lie, the Nazis encouraged their victims to pack belongings. Sometimes they even had them get tickets before boarding the trains.

38

The Jews from western Europe often traveled in passenger coaches to the killing centers. But the Nazis packed their Polish victims into freight cars and cattle cars—without toilets. Vicious guards screamed at the passengers, hit them with rifles, and shot many. Victims received no food or water, sometimes for days. In the closed cars, many died from the heat and lack of air. The guards shot anyone trying to escape.[19]

Nazis chose Poland as the site of their death camps because Jews lived in nearby ghettos and the efficient railroad system made it easy to transport victims quickly. This group of Hungarian Jews arrived at the Auschwitz-Birkenau ramp in Poland in 1944. The Nazis are shown selecting who would go to the labor camps (and live) and who would go to the death camps (and die).

When the transports arrived at the killing centers, the passengers quickly realized what was going on.

The smell told us all, the horrible smell of burning human flesh. They were shouting orders. "Get undressed! Line up here." They were shaving off people's hair. . . . The whole situation was so totally unreal, we were laughing, crying and laughing.[20]

The Nazis forced their victims to strip. Then they made them turn over any valuables they had brought along. To the end, the Nazis lied to the victims about their fate. Guards told them they were going to shower, to get rid of lice. In some camps, the Jews were given soap and assured that nothing would hurt them. Breathe deeply, the guards told their victims, it will strengthen your lungs.[21] Then they marched them to the "showers"— which, of course, were not showers at all. Poison gas, rather than water, filled the crowded death chambers.

Later, inmates who had been selected to help the S.S. pulled out bodies. Next they checked mouths of the corpses for gold teeth. Dentists knocked them out. Then inmates dragged the bodies into giant furnaces, also built by German industry. After the bodies were burned, inmates went through the ashes to find any remaining gold teeth.

Eventually, the victims' gold was sent on to German banks and credited to Nazi accounts. This "blood money" could then be used for the German war effort. They also gathered huge loads of personal belongings. Victims' watches and pens were passed out to soldiers. Their clothing was donated to German aid societies. Some of this property was never distributed. After the war, warehouses were discovered with hundreds of

These children were kept alive in the Auschwitz II (Birkenau)
concentration camp. They stand between two rows of barbed-wire
fences awaiting their fate after liberation.

thousands of men's suits, women's outfits, shoes, eyeglasses, false teeth, and many other items.[22] Many of these things can now be found at the United States Holocaust Memorial Museum in Washington, D.C.

The Nazis built killing factories within some of their work camps, too. Auschwitz concentration camp had the most modern and deadly killing center of all.[23] At Auschwitz, slave labor and mass murder went hand in hand. This system was efficient: Inmates who weakened could be sent directly to the gas chambers at Birkenau. Sick workers could be replaced quickly with other slaves.

The killing centers did their job, as the number of victims shows:

VICTIMS OF THE KILLING CENTERS	
Auschwitz	2,000,000
Belzec	600,000
Chelmno	340,000
Majdanek	1,380,000
Sobibor	250,000
Treblinka	800,000
TOTAL:	5,370,000[24]

By the time the extermination camps shut down in late 1944, the Nazis were about to lose World War II. But their hidden battlefront against the Jews had proved successful beyond belief.

4

The Other Victims

"Jews kaput, Gypsies too; and then the Ukranians, then comes you. "[1]

The Nazis were obsessed with the idea of racial purity. At the top of their racial scale were "pure" Germans. Hitler called them Aryans. He preached that the Aryans were a master race. These blond-haired, blue-eyed Germans, he promised, would conquer the world.

Hitler planned to create a huge German empire in Eastern Europe. He called his plan *Lebensraum*—or "living space." His plan was to rid Eastern Europe of Jews, Slavs, and other so-called "inferior" people. Then the rich farmlands of Eastern Europe could be free for his master race.

The dark-skinned, dark-haired Slavs of Eastern Europe fell near the bottom of the Nazi racial scale.

This Jewish boy stands in his ghetto selling armbands with the star of David. Jews weren't the only people the Nazis tried to persecute. Hitler wanted to rid Eastern Europe of all so-called "inferior people"—including Slavs, Gypsies, and the handicapped.

Russians, Czechs, Poles, Slovenes, Croats, Slovaks, and Serbs are all Slavic people. Hitler considered them subhuman—not much better than animals. The Nazis also despised the sick, people with handicaps, homosexuals, and Gypsies. At the very bottom of Hitler's racial scale were the Jews. To the Nazis, the Jews counted less than insects. Over time, Hitler hoped to eliminate all of these undesirable groups from German "living space."[2]

As Hitler's army moved into Eastern Europe, the invaders began carrying out his plan. They starved, murdered, and abused civilians. They sent strong, young people to Germany to work as slave laborers. Under the Nazi slave-labor program, 5 million workers from all over Europe were brought to Germany against their will.[3]

Many civilians were forced from their homes. The Nazis sent them to holding areas and concentration camps. In Poland, five hundred thousand Germans took over places from which civilians had been removed.[4]

The Nazis' first victims were political opponents. This group included Socialists, Communists, Social Democrats, and labor unionists. After the war started, resistance fighters also ended up in the camps. In fact, any Germans who resisted the Nazis could become victims. Thousands of Jehovah's Witnesses, priests, and freethinkers ended up in concentration camps.

The Nazis used colored cloth triangles to identify concentration camp prisoners. Colors and shapes varied from camp to camp, but there were basic camp colors.

In the camps, Jews also wore a second triangle, usually red, that formed the Star of David—the Jewish star—with the yellow triangle on top.[5]

CLOTH TRIANGLE COLORS	
yellow:	Jew
brown:	Gypsy
green	criminal
mauve:	Jehovah's Witness
pink:	homosexual
red:	political
black:	asocial
blue:	emigré

By the end of the war, the Nazis had killed at least 6 million non-Jews. By some estimates as many as many as 13 million non-Jews were murdered under Hitler's Third Reich. In other words, the total number of civilians and prisoners of war who died at the hand of the Nazis was as many as 19 million.[6]

People with Handicaps

Hitler considered people with handicaps defective. He did not want their offspring polluting his master race. As early as 1933, Nazis began sterilizing people with handicaps. Anyone who suffered from physical or mental problems, deafness, blindness, or alcoholism would be prevented from having children.[7]

By 1939, Hitler had turned to a quicker method of dealing with the people of Germany who had handicaps. He set up the Reich Committee for Scientific Research of Heredity and Severe Constitutional Diseases. The Nazis often used fake science or fake medicine to justify brutality and murder. This committee was really just a cover for killing five thousand deformed or retarded children. Sadly, many German doctors went along. The Nazis called their program mercy killing.[8]

Another top secret program of mercy killing was known as T-4. With the help of German doctors, the Nazis gathered together people with mental or emotional problems. Buses with blacked-out windows transported these people to several killing centers. At each killing center, victims were led to a room that looked like a shower. Poison gas was then piped into the fake shower room. Afterward, the bodies were burned. The ashes were sent in urns to the victims' families. Families also received condolence letters saying that their loved ones had died of natural causes.

Word of the secret killing centers leaked out. Some families received more than one urn of ashes. People living near the killing centers saw smoke coming from the crematoria where the bodies were burned. Children raced after the buses with the blacked-out windows. They shouted: "There's the murder-box coming again."[9]

Many Germans, including Catholic and Protestant clergy, protested. Finally, Hitler stopped the T-4 program. But the Nazis had already killed between eighty and one hundred thousand people with handicaps.[10]

The T-4 program served as a kind of experiment for the Nazis. In these killing centers, the Nazis perfected efficient methods for mass murder. The poison gas chambers, the fake showers, and the crematoria all reappeared later in the Nazi death camps. German doctors continued to play a part in the ongoing mass murder.

Gypsies

Like the Jews, the Gypsies had long been outsiders in Europe. They were a dark-skinned people, whose ancestors came from India. Although they had lived in Europe for hundreds of years, they had their own customs and culture.

Also like the Jews, the Gypsies had suffered prejudice through the centuries. In the 1500s, Eastern Europeans made them slaves. In the 1600s, people hunted Gypsies like animals. There were many countries that passed laws to keep them out.[11]

The Nazis did not invent persecution against the Gypsies. But they built on old hatreds. They made the Gypsies special targets of their abuse.

To justify their plans for the Gypsies, the Nazis turned to their fake science. German doctors carried out phony experiments to show that Gypsies were defective. The head of this so-called research was Robert Ritter, a German psychiatrist. Ritter ran the Reich Office for Race and Hygiene Population Biology. He sent out researchers to measure Gypsy skulls. His researchers charted Gypsy eye color. They made wax face masks to study Gypsy features. They even devised tests to show that Gypsy blood was different from other blood. Based on these fake experiments, the Nazis claimed that Gypsies were criminal by nature. They also said that their research proved that Gypsies were primitive.[12]

By 1938, the Nazis were rounding up Gypsies. They dragged men, women, and children from their houses and workplaces. Many were sent to concentration camps

48

Gypsies were special targets of Nazi abuse. Because of prejudices that were centuries old, it was easy for the Nazis to build on long-standing hatreds.

and holding areas. Others were simply murdered by killing squads.

"The fascists hunted Gypsies as if they were game," one Ukrainian remembered.[13]

Anton Fojn was a Gypsy taken from his home during a raid.

> My father had been picked up in an earlier raid on Bruck an der Mur. At the railroad station, he found out that my uncle and I had been taken. He asked the Germans to let us travel in the same boxcar. Two days later, June 28, the train stopped just outside the gates of Dachau. We waited, locked in the airless boxcar for about three quarters of an hour. Then we heard a shout as thirty or forty young S.S. men unlocked the bolts and threw open the doors. "Austrian pigheads," they screamed. "Out, out. Run, . . . run." Their whips fell on us, killing two men as we ran toward the gates of Dachau. . . .
>
> Little did I know that I would consider Dachau heaven compared to Buchenwald. In Buchenwald, everything had to be done on the run. *"Schnell, schnell* [faster, faster]," the guards shouted as we struggled to haul trees or dig trenches. Blows fell on our backs and necks. One of my uncles could not move quickly enough. An S.S. man bludgeoned him to death.[14]

In the concentration camps, Gypsies were abused, starved, and gassed. The Nazis continued to use Gypsies in terrifying and painful medical experiments. They tested Cyklon B, a poison gas, on 250 Gypsy children in

1940. Soon they were using that poison in the gas chambers of their extermination camps.

In 1900, an estimated 1 million Gypsies lived in Europe.[15] By the end of the war, the Nazis had killed three to five hundred thousand Gypsies.[16]

Jehovah's Witnesses

Jehovah's Witnesses are members of a devout Christian group. They do not enlist in armed forces or fight in wars. They see themselves as God's soldiers. Members of this group also believe in spreading their message about Christianity. They try to convert others to their religion.

In Hitler's Germany, there were only about twenty to twenty-five thousand Jehovah's Witnesses. But they enraged the Nazis. They refused to join the German army. They spoke out against Hitler, saying that he was evil. They never said, "*Heil Hitler.*" Nor would they salute the Nazi flag. Moreover, Jehovah's Witnesses continued to pass out newspapers and books carrying their message.

In 1937, the Nazis began persecuting Jehovah's Witnesses. They prohibited Jehovah's Witnesses from meeting or praying together. They carried out searches for their banned literature. About one out of four Jehovah's Witnesses ended up in a concentration camp or prison. These prisoners could easily have gotten released. All they had to do was sign an oath, saying they would not meet with other members of their group. In concentration camps, Jehovah's Witnesses were abused and forced to do hard labor. Others were shot. Many died. But very few signed the Nazi oath.[17]

51

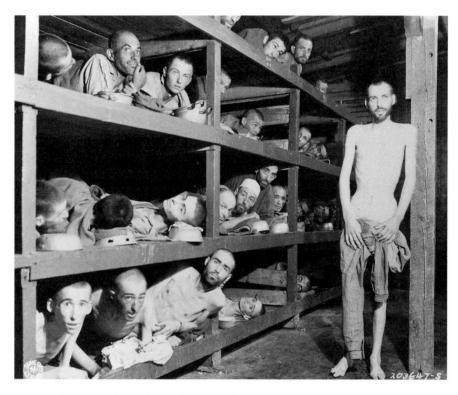

These are slave laborers in the Buchenwald camp where Anton Fojn and his family went after Dachau. Many people at this camp died of malnutrition.

Homosexuals

In pre-Nazi Germany, homosexuality was against the law. Nevertheless, homosexuals were tolerated. There were many gay bars, and pro-gay writing was published during the two decades before the Third Reich.

With Hitler's rise to power, the Nazis cracked down on homosexuals. Homosexuals stood in the way of their wish to improve the German race. They raided gay bars. They destroyed books defending homosexuality. They sent between ten and fifteen thousand homosexuals to concentration camps.[18]

In the camps, the "pink triangles" received brutal treatment. Many homosexuals slaved in the rock quarries. The Nazis also carried out their fake research on homosexuals. They said they wanted to find out whether homosexuality was inherited. They injected homosexual inmates with male hormones. Eventually, they offered homosexuals their freedom, if they would agree to be castrated or submit themselves to sexual abuse and prostitution. Under these conditions, an estimated six to nine thousand homosexual inmates died in the camps.[19]

Slavic People

Many Slavic people lived in Czechoslovakia, Poland, the Ukraine, and other countries occupied by the Nazis. The Nazis looked down on the Slavs as unintelligent and primitive. According to Hitler's plan, they would send one third of the Slavic people to Asia, murder one third, and keep one third as slaves. As a result, Slavs were not

53

killed automatically. In Czechoslovakia, where the Nazis were met with no resistance, most Slavs were spared.

According to the Nazis, certain groups of Slavs were especially dangerous. In Poland, priests, professors, doctors, lawyers, writers, and rulers were tortured and murdered. In some areas, half the priests and lawyers were killed. They also murdered almost half of all Poland's doctors and professors. The Nazis reasoned that, without leaders, Poles would not oppose them.[20]

The Nazis threw civilians out of their homes. They crowded them onto cold train cars without food, water, or even enough air. They dumped many people at railroad stations or in open fields. Others ended up in Germany, working as slave laborers in factories.

Those left behind might have been killed or arrested at any time. The Nazis shut down Polish schools and churches. Polish children could only go to school through the fourth grade. The Nazis also destroyed Polish statues, art, monuments, and libraries. As Hitler's army moved into the Ukraine and the European parts of Russia, similar scenes were repeated.

The Nazis also mistreated the 5.7 million Slavs who surrendered from the Soviet army. These men were starved and forced into hard labor. Over 3 million died in Nazi custody. By comparison, few British or American prisoners died as Nazi war prisoners.[21]

By the end of the war, Poland had lost about 3 million non-Jewish civilians. So had the Ukraine. In Belorussia, the death toll was one of every four citizens; an estimated 2.3 million people died. The Ukranian city of Kiev lost half of its population.[22]

5

Rescuers

Many non-Jews turned their backs on their Jewish neighbors. Some refused to help. Some did nothing or pretended not to know what was happening. Others helped the Nazis. They turned over Jews to German authorities. They betrayed neighbors who were hiding Jews. Some even participated in the mass murdering.

Anti-Semitism and greed motivated many who helped the Nazis. Helping the Nazi effort could lead to favors from the Nazis. Informers sometimes received money for their dirty work. In Poland, people turned in their Jewish neighbors for scarce sugar.

But many people who did nothing to help the Jews were simply scared. Their fear is understandable: Anybody hiding a Jew might be sent to a concentration camp, hung, or shot on the spot.

In the face of the *Einsatzgruppen,* the mayor of Kremenchug, Senitsa Vershovsky, tried to help the Jews.

The Nazis shot him. It is not known exactly how many other rescuers died along with the Jews they tried to save.

Jan Karski, who spied for the Polish underground, recalled:

> Now, to help a Jew during the war was very dangerous. In France or Belgium you might go to jail if they caught you. . . . But in Eastern Europe, particularly Poland, instantaneous death! Execution! Sometimes if the family was involved, the entire family shot![1]

Despite the huge risk, non-Jews did help throughout Germany and occupied Europe. Some people gave money. Others provided temporary hiding places or helped Jews escape to safer zones. Still others left food near places where Jews were hiding. After the Warsaw ghetto was burned, some Jews hid in sewers. Polish sympathizers brought them supplies.

Many people passed information to Jewish leaders, underground groups, or officials who could help. In Bulgaria, for instance, Liliana Fanitsa worked as secretary to the man who set up the "Commissariat for the Jewish Problem." When Fanitsa learned of his plan to deport Bulgarian Jews in early March 1943, she warned leaders of the Jewish community. The Bulgarian government decided to postpone the deportation. In the end, Bulgaria was one of the few European countries where most of the Jews survived.[2]

During the Nazi terror, many sympathetic officials passed out falsified papers. Such documentation often meant the difference between life and death. The right papers could provide safe passage from occupied German

This Polish woman is being sent to execution for helping the Jews. Translated, the sign around her neck says, "For selling merchandise to Jews."

lands. Or they could allow Jews to pass as Christians. From April through June 1944, Nazis deported over four hundred thousand Hungarian Jews to concentration camps. Angelo Roncalli was a Catholic official in Hungary, who later became Pope John XXIII. He was asked to help the Jews. Roncalli authorized the baptism of thousands of Jews in Budapest's air-raid shelters. Catholic baptismal certificates then served as passports of escape.[3]

Other falsified papers made Jews overnight citizens of neutral countries. Raoul Wallenberg worked in the Hungarian embassy. This Swedish aristocrat gave citizenship papers to thousands of Jews. He also bought housing for his new Swedish "citizens." Sweden was neutral during the war. Therefore, the Nazis considered Wallenberg's property neutral territory, even though it was in Hungary. As a result, his housing served as a sanctuary, too. Wallenberg's efforts saved at least seventy thousand Jews.[4]

Many government officers allowed refugees to cross their closed borders. Aristedes de Sousa Mendes was a Portuguese government official in southern France. Against orders, he gave out visas to help Jews escape into Portugal. He turned his home into a sanctuary. But his government discouraged these activities. Eventually, they even took away his job and pension. In response, he said, "I cannot but act as a Christian."[5]

Like Mendes, many people hid their hunted neighbors, in some cases for days, in other cases for years. They hid them in convents, in farmhouses, in spare rooms, in basements or attics, behind walls, under floors, even in holes in the ground. Of the Netherland's one hundred forty thousand Jews, about twenty-five thousand went into hiding. A small group of trusted friends rescued Anne Frank, her family, and four others. For two years, the Frank family lived in rooms above Otto Frank's former office.[6]

Unlike the Franks, most families could not hide together in one place. Many Jews moved from one hideout to another. Often, family members were separated from each other. Many parents were forced to leave their children with strangers. Some families on the run simply left their babies or young children—and prayed for the best. A crying baby might jeopardize a whole group of Jews trying to hide. But, Jewish children could sometimes pass as family members or cousins in Christian homes.

Why did certain non-Jews take their hunted neighbors into their homes, while others turned their backs? When asked, some rescuers mention their religious faith. Others talk about their upbringing or a wonderful relative who influenced them. Many say they simply did what came naturally—helping those in need. As John Weidner, who organized a French rescue network, put it:

> I saw a group of Jewish women and children who had been arrested and who were being deported to the east. One woman had a baby in her arms. The baby started to cry and make a lot of noise in the railroad station. The S.S. officer who was in charge ordered the woman to make the baby stop crying, but she could not do it. In a rage, the officer took the baby out of the arms of that woman, smashed the baby on the floor, and crushed its head. We heard the wail of that mother. It was something terrible. And all the while, the S.S. officers stood around laughing.

> When I saw such things happening to the Jewish
> people, it was something so opposed to my concept
> of life, to all that I was taught to believe that I felt it
> was my duty in conscience to help these people.[10]

Rescuers like Weidner, Fanitsa, Wallenberg, and Souza Mendez came from all stations in life. Some were high-level government officials. Some were rich aristocrats. Others were businessmen. But most were common people with uncommon courage. The following accounts are just a few of those that came to light after the war. They stand for the many unsung tales of courage during a dark time.

Leokadia Jarmirska

Leokadia Jarmirska lived alone in a small Polish town near Warsaw. The Gestapo, the Nazi secret police, had arrested her husband for carrying an illegal newspaper. Jarmirska made a meager living in a warehouse run by the Germans.

One day, she left her job early. On her way home, she noticed a group of women, standing near a store where she shopped. When she stepped closer, she saw a small girl, not much more than a year old. The girl was crying, "Mama, Mama."

She was a Jewish child, Jarmirska realized. Jarmirska took the baby home, fed her, and put her to bed. From that day on, she treated the little girl she called Bogusia as her own.

When the fighting neared Warsaw, Jarmirska left with some neighbors for a safer place. She carried Bogusia on her back for many miles. They slept in barns and had no hot food for days.

Anne Frank: Lost Hopes, Lost Dreams

You have probably heard of Anne Frank. Her diary is one of the world's most well-known books. Over 20 million copies have been sold.[7] Anne Frank wrote it during World War II, mostly while she was in hiding with her family in Amsterdam, the Netherlands. She and her family were trying to escape from the Nazis.

A few weeks after Anne's thirteenth birthday, the Frank family joined the van Pels family in the "secret annex," as they called their hiding place. During her two years in hiding, Anne wrote in her diary. She described the people living in the secret annex. She told about her conflicts with her mother and sister, and about everyday life in hiding. She shared her fears about being discovered and her sadness about all she had lost. She discussed her hopes for the future, including her dream of becoming a famous writer some day. Through her ordeal, Anne maintained the belief that "people are really good at heart."[8]

On August 4, 1944, the Nazis raided the secret annex. They sent Anne and her sister Margo to Bergen-Belsen concentration camp. Both girls died in March, 1945, a few weeks before British soldiers liberated the camp.[9]

Today, Anne Frank's diary reminds everyone who reads it of all the hopes, dreams, creativity, and goodness that were lost during the Holocaust.

After the war finally ended, Jarmirska's husband returned. By a miracle, so did Bogusia's father. Even more amazing, he tracked down Jarmirska. Both men had survived concentration camps. As for Jarmirska, she had cared for Bogusia for three years. She had protected the child with her life. Now she had to face the prospect of losing the little girl. For a few years, all four lived together. But the two men could not get along. Both had suffered too much in the camps. Finally, Bogusia's father took her to Israel. Leokadia Jarmirska never fully recovered from the loss.[11]

Herman Graebe

Herman Graebe was a German construction engineer who worked for a construction firm. In 1941, his company sent him to Sdolbonov, Poland, to build a railroad facility.

A few weeks after Graebe arrived in Sdolbonov, he witnessed a massacre in nearby Dubno. He watched as German soldiers forced men, women, and children to undress. He saw the soldiers move these naked prisoners into a pit and shoot them. Before seeing the killing units with his own eyes, Graebe hadn't believed the stories of their butchery. But as he watched, his outrage grew. He thought of his own son, only nine or ten years old. Herman Graebe realized that his boy might ask him one day, "What did you do during the war?" What would he answer?[12]

Graebe began using his position to hire hundreds of Jews for his firm. He protected his workers with work papers. He provided medical care, food, and transit visas. He also passed on information that might save lives.

Herman Graebe helped to save the lives of over three hundred Jews.[13]

Oskar Schindler

Oskar Schindler was a German-Catholic businessman. During World War II, he moved to occupied Poland. He hoped to make a fortune off the war. A member of the Nazi party, he took over a factory in Kraków. Some Jews worked as slave laborers in this factory. Schindler moved into large quarters. He lived a life of luxury.

But soon Schindler grew disgusted with the cruelty and greed of the Nazis. Sometimes he learned in advance of their plans to terrorize the Jews. He passed warnings to Jewish leaders. At his own expense, he gave his Jewish workers extra food. Soon his factory became known as a safe place. Jews who had factory jobs with Schindler were less likely to be murdered or sent to death camps. Schindler hired more and more Jews. He put himself in danger, declaring that unqualified workers were "essential" to his factory. In fact, many of his workers were too young, too old, or untrained and of no great use. But he was determined to save them all.

At one point, his workers were deported to Auschwitz. Schindler stepped in, paying huge amounts of money to get them back. As he learned of deportation plans in other places, Schindler passed warnings to Jewish leaders. Several times, Schindler ended up in prison himself. Each time, the contacts he had made, mostly through bribes, came to his rescue.

At the end of the war, his workers were liberated. To thank him, they made Schindler a gold ring. In it, they wrote the Hebrew words that mean, "He who saves one life, saves a whole world."

Le Chambon-sur-Lignon

Le Chambon-sur-Lignon is a small Protestant village in south-central France. During the war, many Jewish refugees fled there and found help. The rescue effort began with the Protestant pastor, Andre Trocmé, and his wife, Magda. A poor woman came to the door and Magda Trocmé let her in. As it turned out, the woman was a German Jew looking for shelter, and the pastor's wife told her, "Naturally, come in, come in."[14]

Following the example of the minister and his wife, the villagers began taking refugees into their homes and farms, too. Soon there were Jews all over Le Chambon.

Andre Trocmé volunteered to go into the concentration camps in southern France to care for the children. These were not death camps, but many people died of starvation there. The pastor was asked instead to hide rescued prisoners in his village. A group of children from the camps found a safe place in Le Chambon. They received food and shelter. They went to school with village children. At times, local farmers would hide the Jews in the countryside.

Eventually, French police came and took Trocmé to a detention camp. The villagers found out and began dropping off small gifts of support for him. Their gifts included a piece of soap, a candle, and a roll of toilet paper on which verses of the Bible had been written, for encouragement.[15]

After the war, people praised the villagers of Le Chambon for their courage. But the villagers themselves

This group photo was taken at Le Chambon-sur-Lignon in France where many villagers took refugees into their homes.

were modest about their deeds. As Lesley Maber, who lived in Le Chambon from 1939 to 1982 explained: ". . . the reaction was—and still is—'Why all the fuss? It was only natural.'"[16]

Adelaide Hautval

Even in the death camps there were people who risked their lives to help others. Dr. Adelaide Hautval was one of these rescuers. In occupied France, she protested vehemently against the cruel treatment of Jews. As a result, the Gestapo sent her to Auschwitz. She ended up in an area where Dr. Mengele conducted his horrible experiments on inmates. She refused to cooperate. During a typhoid epidemic, Hautval hid and nursed patients who would otherwise have been gassed. For her kindness, the inmates called her "The Angel in White" and "The Saint." To her fellow sufferers, she said, "Here we are all condemned to death. Let us behave like human beings as long as we are alive."[17]

Denmark, Finland, Bulgaria, and Italy

The fate of Jews differed widely from country to country in occupied Europe. The Nazis wiped out the Jews of Poland, Hungary, and Czechoslovakia. In Poland, 90 percent died. But over 95 percent of Denmark's Jews survived. The survival rate was also high for the Jews of Italy, Bulgaria, and Finland.[18]

There were many reasons for these differences. But one important factor was the attitude of the people in each country. Eastern Europe had a long history of vicious anti-Semitism. Denmark and Finland, by contrast, had long been tolerant of the Jews. For over two thousand years, the Jews had lived in Italy. In all of these countries an underground—a group of people working secretly to defeat the Nazis—helped to pass on Nazi plans for killing the Jews. Based on such information, rescue efforts were carried out in Bulgaria, Finland, and Denmark.[19]

Italy was Germany's ally in World War II. But Italians did not cooperate with the Nazi's "final solution." They refused to carry out racial laws or to deport Italian Jews. In 1943, Germany occupied Italy. During the roundup that followed, many Italians protected the Jews. Some hid Jews and helped them escape. Others gave out fake papers. Many Jews found safety in monasteries, convents, and churches. The Italian army also aided Jews.[20]

When the Nazi occupation started, many Danes organized for resistance. They collected weapons. They set up an illegal printing press. They also carried out strikes, sabotage, and even riots. In 1943, news arrived that the Germans planned to round up Danish Jews on Rosh Hashanah, the Jewish New Year and holy day. The source of this information was George Ferdinand Ducckwitz, a German naval officer.

The Danish people responded quickly. Through a coordinated effort, they ferried the Jews across the water to safety in neutral Sweden. Most Danish citizens helped. They contributed food, money, hiding places, and boats. The rescue effort went on for two weeks. It did not end after 7,220 Danish Jews had escaped. The Danes continued to protect Jewish property, homes, and even their pets and plants, until the owners returned.

Rescue efforts were carried out in Denmark when the Danish first heard news of the Nazi plans for killing the Jews. Here, Danish fishermen ferry a boatload of Jewish fugitives across a narrow sound to neutral Sweden. Within just a few weeks of the first arrests by the Germans in 1943, some seven thousand Danish Jews managed to make their way to the safety of fishing boats that used this route.

The government also gave new homes and apartments to those who lost them.[21]

In Israel, on a Jerusalem hillside sits Yad Vashem. Yad Vashem is a memorial to those who died and those who fought to save lives during the Holocaust. It includes a museum, a pillar of Heroism, a synagogue, a Hall of Remembrance, a Hall of Names, and a center for Holocaust research. Along the path leading up to Yad Vashem and on the knoll behind it are many trees. These carob trees were all planted in honor of non-Jews who risked their lives to save Jews during the Holocaust. In Hebrew these heroes are called the *Hasidei Umot HaOlam*—the "Righteous Among Nations of the World."

As of 1993, over ten thousand people have been honored at Yad Vashem as *Hasidei Umot HaOlam.*[22]

69

6

The Liberation and After

As Allied troops advanced toward the occupied countries, the Nazis tried to cover up evidence of their crimes at the death camps. They blew up gas chambers. They burned the storerooms holding the inmates' stolen belongings. They destroyed records. They planted trees and buried bodies to hide their mass murders. They sent prisoners on death marches, away from the camps, away from the troops that might free them. During these long marches, many sick, starving inmates died. Those who could not keep up were shot. Finally, though, time ran out for the Nazis.

Soviet soldiers were the first to liberate the death camps. On July 23, 1944, they liberated Majdanek, outside Lublin, Poland. Soviet journalists and photographers reported the grim facts: gas chambers where 250 people had died at a time; a storehouse with eight hundred thousand shoes; one thousand people clinging to life.[1]

70

Most of the world, however, refused to believe the Soviet reports. The Germans called them propaganda; they claimed that the Russians were spreading these stories in order to damage the Nazis. At first, the Allies agreed that the Soviet stories were exaggerated. But they would soon discover that these reports were true and were only a small part of the gruesome reality.

On April 5, 1945, American scouts from the Fourth Armored Division discovered Ohrdruf labor camp, a subcamp of Buchenwald. It was a small camp, the first of many liberated by the Americans and British. The soldiers found piles of corpses, tools of torture and death, and walking skeletons.

After viewing the camp, General Dwight D. Eisenhower ordered all American troops in the area to tour Ohrdruf. "We are told that the American soldier does not know what he is fighting for," he said. "Now, at least, he will know what he is fighting *against*."[2]

The British entered Bergen-Belsen on April 15. They found sixty thousand prisoners barely holding on to life.[3] Thousands of unburied bodies littered the grounds. A typhus epidemic raged. News reports, photographs, and films of the newly liberated camp circulated around the world. Gradually, the horror of what the Nazis had done began to sink in—and to be acknowledged by the rest of the world.

During April, Americans liberated Buchenwald, Nordhausen, Ohrdruf, Landsberg, Woebelein, Gunskirchen, Ebensee, Flossenburg, and Dachau.[4] The troops were shocked at what they saw.

71

Oh the odors, well there is no way to describe the odors . . . there were combat men who had been all the way through on the invasion—were ill and vomiting, throwing up, just the sight of this.[5]

—C.W. Doughty, liberator of Nordhausen

The first thing I saw was a stack of bodies that appeared to be about, oh, 20 feet long and about, oh, as high as a man could reach, which looked like cordwood stacked up there, and the thing I'll never forget was the fact that closer inspection found people whose eyes were still blinking maybe three or four deep inside the stack.[6]

—Jack Hallett, liberator of Dachau

We were all accustomed to seeing death. But when you see a poor guy so wasted away that you could practically read a newspaper through him, that's another matter.[7]

—Herb Butt, liberator of Dachau

In early May, American troops entered Mauthausen and Gusen. A few days later, the war ended. Now began the battle of caring for survivors and burying the dead. In many areas, townspeople were forced to view the camps and help bury bodies. They dug trenches and carried corpses to mass graves. Troops distributed food, water, and medicine to survivors. Near some camps, teams of physicians and nurses set up shop. From other camps, soldiers evacuated survivors to hospitals—or evicted civilians from their homes and turned the housing into clinics or apartments for survivors.

Prisoners with contagious diseases, such as typhus, diphtheria, and tuberculosis, had to be isolated. Some

When the British entered Bergen-Belsen, they found sixty thousand
prisoners barely holding onto life. This photo was taken on April 20
of some unfortunate people who did not survive.

inmates suffered from infections. Others needed special diets. Some survivors were so sickly and thin that they had to be fed liquids through special tubes.

Despite efforts to help them, many victims could not survive the first weeks of liberation. At Mauthausen, for example, at least two hundred inmates died every day.[8] The story was similar in Dachau with about one hundred forty prisoners dying each day.[9] By the end of June, medical rescue efforts began paying off. At Mauthausen, the death rate fell to between five and fifteen a week.[10]

Displaced Persons

Eventually, prisoners began making their way home—if they had homes. At war's end, as many as 30 million people were stranded away from their homelands. Many had nowhere to go.[11] These displaced persons, or DPs as they were called, included Jews, Gypsies, political prisoners, and slave laborers of many nationalities.

Some DPs did not want to return to their old lands. Many Poles, for instance, feared going back to a now Communist Poland. Many Eastern European Jews had lost everything in the Holocaust—family, housing, careers. There was nothing to return to. They also feared new waves of anti-Semitism in their old countries. Their fears were justifiable as civilians had already attacked and murdered some Jewish survivors returning home.

Many DPs ended up for a time in DP camps—old army barracks, slave labor camps, and the like. Conditions varied but were often very poor. Many camps were crowded and unsanitary. In some, DPs were still held like prisoners behind barbed wire fences with little to do.

Survivors of the Mauthausen camp cheer soldiers of the United States Army two days after their liberation. Translated, the banner in the background reads, "The Spanish Anti-Fascists Salute the Liberating Forces."

Those overseeing the DPs were not always mindful of their needs or fears.

In August 1945, President Harry S. Truman sent Earl Harrison of the state department to report on DP camp conditions. Harrison's sympathetic report led to some changes in the DP camps.[12]

With time, most DPs were resettled. Many Jewish survivors made new homes in Western Europe, the United States, South America, Australia, and South Africa. Others moved to Palestine (which includes present-day Israel) in the hopes of establishing a Jewish homeland. Israel officially became a state on May 14, 1948.

The Nuremberg Trials

At the end of World War II, much of Europe was in ruins. Hitler's dreams of world conquest had brought death to 35 million people. Nazi efforts to wipe out all of Europe's Jews had nearly succeeded. Undeniable proof of mass murder, slave labor, torture, and brutality had shocked the world. Now the world demanded punishment for the Nazis.[13] Hitler killed himself on April 30, 1945, as United States, British, and Soviet troops closed in to liberate Germany.

In fact, the Allies had already decided to punish Nazi leaders two years before the end of World War II. At that time, reports of Nazi brutality were pouring out of the occupied countries. On October 26, 1943, the United Nations War Crimes Commission met in London for the first time. This commission helped to collect evidence of war crimes and to determine who was responsible for these crimes.[14]

The war crimes trial began on October 6, 1945, in Nuremberg, Germany. The Allies chose this site because it had been the Nazis' spiritual capital. In Nuremberg, the Nazis had held huge rallies. They had cheered Hitler's hate-filled speeches. In Nuremberg, they had passed the Nuremberg Laws, wiping out the rights of German Jews.[15]

The Allies charged twenty-four Nazi leaders and six Nazi organizations. The charges took four hours to read. The perpetrators were accused of the following types of crimes:

Crimes against peace: Planning, preparing, and waging a war that violated previous treaties and agreements.

War Crimes: Violating the customs of war by murdering, mistreating, deporting, and enslaving civilians and prisoners of war; and destroying cities, towns, and villages without military purpose.

Crimes against humanity: murdering, mistreating, enslaving, deporting, and persecuting civilians for religious, racial, or political reasons.[16]

The trials lasted nearly one year, until October 1, 1946. All of the defendants, except for two, pleaded "not guilty." They argued that they were following orders.

At one point during the trial, the prosecution showed a documentary film of the Nazi concentration camps as they were found during liberation. When the lights turned on again, the judges left in disgust. The defendants sat in silence.[17]

Of the twenty-four defendants originally sentenced to stand trial, one committed suicide and one elderly defendant never came to trial because he was too ill and not likely to recover. Twelve were sentenced to death, three to life imprisonment, and four to long prison terms. Three were found not guilty.[18]

Since the Nuremberg trials, many other Nazis have been tried for their crimes. At the end of the twentieth century, Nazi hunters continue to discover a few of the old Nazi leaders. There is no statute of limitations for crimes against humanity. This means that Nazi criminals can be brought to trial, and punished regardless of how much time has passed since they committed their crimes.

Survivors

For victims of the Holocaust, the effects of this terror did not end with the Nuremberg trials. The trauma of abuse and mistreatment remain as scars that will never fade. As one Jewish victim who lost home and family put it, "To be a survivor of the Holocaust means that your heart is broken. It might mend a little bit, but it could never be complete."[19]

Many survivors went on to build new lives with new families, new homes, new careers. Some worked to educate the world about what had happened in Nazi Germany. Others chose not to talk about their terrible experiences. Many others found that the rest of the world didn't want to hear their stories or didn't care. For most victims of the Holocaust, however, the traumatic events still linger as heavy burdens that they can never really lay to rest. Many still have vivid nightmares—of dogs barking, of German soldiers chasing them, of Nazis screaming "Dirty Jews." Others, still traumatized by the starvation diet of the camps, wake up at night and need

Survivors of the Bergen-Belsen camp walk along a camp street next to large heaps of rubble that may very well consist of the personal belongings of inmates.

to eat. Still others fear loud noises, such as a telephone ringing or children talking too loudly.

Over time, some survivors and their children have built organizations dedicated to preserving the memory of the Holocaust. Groups like the American Gathering of Jewish Holocaust Survivors have held commemoration ceremonies, including a huge service in New York City to mark the fiftieth anniversary of the liberation of the concentration camps. Thousands of survivors attended this ceremony along with President Clinton and other politicians. A Boston-based group, One Generation After, holds an annual Holocaust Remembrance service and sponsors awareness groups, an oral history project, newsletters, and a speakers bureau. Yet another group, New York's Self-help, a nonprofit organization founded by survivors, holds an annual Christmas party for AIDS families. Their members understand the pain of families torn apart.[20]

Still, many survivors and their children wonder what it would be like to celebrate holidays with a large family. Said Ira Kolin, whose mother, Stella, was the only member of her family to survive the Holocaust, "We're a very small family now. I never had a grandmother or uncles. When we lost our families, we lost their lives and all the memories that go with it."[21]

7

The Lessons

The Nazi death camps were liberated in April 1945. On May 7, 1945, Germany signed an unconditional surrender at Eisenhower headquarters in Reims, France. World War II was over. The Nazi terror was defeated.

At that time, some people thought both the war and the Holocaust should be left in the past in order to build a new future. Still others thought that the world must never forget.

The Holocaust brought death to millions of innocent men, women, and children. During this whirlwind of destruction, two thirds of Europe's Jews had died. The Nazis also starved, tortured, and enslaved millions of other civilians. In the course of their rampage, they burned villages, stole art and jewelry, and looted the resources of country after country.

Those who say "never forget" feel that the best way to honor those who suffered is to remember the Holocaust and to learn its lessons.

Hate Groups Today

After World War II, some people hoped that the Holocaust would horrify the world so much that all prejudice would end. After the Holocaust, they said, everyone would understand how prejudice leads to murder and destruction—how the Holocaust could happen again, if prejudice didn't end.

These optimists were wrong. Germany outlawed the Nazi party. They banned Hitler's writings. They made it a crime to display Hitler's picture, swastikas, or other Nazi symbols. But outlawing the Nazi party did not put an end to bigotry, anti-Semitism, or racism. In fact, extremists have organized neo-Nazi groups in many countries, Germany included.

These modern-day Nazis spread Hitler's old lies about Jews and other minority groups. They distribute Nazi propaganda and Nazi symbols. They idolize Hitler. Like the Nazis before them, members of these hate groups dream of white supremacy and "final solutions."

In Germany, they go by names such as Free German Workers' Party and the National List. In the United States, they are called the Posse Comitatus, the Order, the White Aryan Resistance, skinheads, and the Ku Klux Klan. And there are many other names. They may have new names, but these groups preach the same old ideas that Adolf Hitler once preached: anti-Semitism, racism, and hate.

What's worse, such groups do not stop with preaching hate or spreading lies. Every year, their members carry out vicious hate crimes. On July 18, 1994, in Buenos Aires, Argentina, a bomb blasted a seven-story

Nazi students unload "un-German" books at the book burning in
1933. Optimists thought that the Holocaust would horrify the
world so much that hate and bigotry would end. Unfortunately,
they were wrong, and events like book burnings still occur today.

building holding two Jewish groups. That blast killed 101 people and injured 200.[1] In February 1995, the Bavarian Liberation Army took responsibility for a series of bombings aimed against Gypsies in Austria.[2]

These two incidents received worldwide attention. But they were not isolated or unique events. In 1993, the FBI reported over seventy-six hundred hate crimes in the United States. That number is up 75 percent since 1991, when forty-five hundred hate crimes were reported. Of those 1993 hate crimes for which information was available, 62 percent were based on race, 18 percent on religion, and 12 percent on sexual orientation.[3]

As for the rest of the world, attacks against Jews rose worldwide between 1993 and 1994, according to the annual report of the World Jewish Congress. In 1993, there were forty-two attacks against Jews *with the intent to murder.* That number increased by thirty to seventy-two in 1994.[4]

Remember the Past

The statistics on hate crimes clearly show that prejudice did not end with the Holocaust. They also clearly show that prejudice can and does lead to violence and murder.

George Santayana, a famous philosopher and historian once wrote, "Those who cannot remember the past are condemned to repeat it."[5] In other words, if people forget the Holocaust and its lessons, such a nightmare could happen again.

Some people would say that so many hate crimes suggest that the world has already begun to forget the Holocaust. The Roper organization polled a group of

American high school students. Their 1993 poll showed that 50 percent of these students did not even know what the Holocaust was. [6]

Yet, the recent civil war in Bosnia has been called a holocaust—or ethnic cleansing, because the mass murders are based on ethnic background and hatred.

Taking a Stand—Together

Fifty years after the Holocaust, it would appear that its memory is beginning to fade. Hate groups spread Hitler's old lies. Hate crimes continue to rise. Many people who survived the horrors of the Holocaust have died. Can anything be done to keep the memory alive and prevent future problems?

One lesson of the Holocaust is that taking action against prejudice does make a difference. During World War II, rescuers saved thousands of lives. Oskar Schindler rescued twelve hundred Jews. Poland today has only four thousand Jewish citizens. [7] Before the war 3.3 million Jews lived there. The Nazis murdered 2.8 million—or 85 percent of the prewar Jewish population in Poland. [8] But six thousand descendants of the *Schlinderjuden*, Schindler's Jews, are alive today. [9]

The rescue at Le Chambon illustrates another important point about fighting prejudice: the power of united action. The villagers of Le Chambon worked together to rescue many people. Their success came, in part, from sharing the effort—and the risk. The Dutch village of Niuvelande also united in support of their Jewish neighbors. Every household hid at least one Jew.

No one feared informers. And Niuvelande villagers found safety in numbers.

On a larger scale, what happened to Europe's Jews varied not only from village to village but also from country to country. Germany's Jews were devastated. Most German citizens fell in line behind the Nazis. Many Germans collaborated, turned in Jews, and committed murder. Many others, fearing for their own lives, turned their backs or ignored the horror. Everyone worried about informers—even within families. Ultimately, nine of ten German Jews died. By contrast, nine of ten Danish Jews survived. Danish citizens stood together against Nazi demands—and the Nazis did not take revenge. Working collectively, the Danes protected their Jews, and very few died.

"Dad, What Did You Do?"

Herman Graebe thought of his son when he saw the mobile killing units at work. He wondered what he would tell his boy one day, when he asked, "Dad, what did you do?"

As it turned out, Graebe could answer his son without shame. He could tell him that he had done what he could to help. He could tell his son that his efforts had saved more than three hundred Jews.[10]

Unfortunately, most Germans today cannot tell their children that they helped. After the war, most citizens claimed that they only learned at war's end about the horrors committed in their backyards. Yet many young Germans today don't believe that it was possible not to know what was going on. Says Nina Rensch, "My grandmother says she didn't know, but I think it's easy to turn your eyes away and not know."[11]

Although some Germans feel that it is time to focus on the future, others disagree. "Germany has now done a lot of thinking about its past," says Daniel Cohn-Bendit, "but it's never enough, compared to what happened."[12]

In fact, many young Germans feel that they, too, must carry the burden for the sins of their parents—or grandparents. As Michael Hueber put it, "German history is my history. I too am guilty in a way. It's important to me to know about what happened and make sure it never happens again."[13]

Don't Wait

As the story of the Holocaust shows, the best time to speak out against bigotry is before the forces of hate grow strong. As philosophers have said, indifference is the real evil. All that is needed for evil to flourish is for good people to do nothing.

All of Germany's churches protested T-4, the Nazi program of "mercy killings" aimed at people with handicaps. These protests had an effect: eventually, Hitler did back down.

Unfortunately, German churches as a group did not protest Hitler's treatment of the Jews. The rest of the world also failed to take united action. The United States called a conference at Evian in France in July 1938, to discuss the refugee problem. But the thirty-two countries attending the conference offered little help for the mostly Jewish refugees fleeing Germany. The Nazis took heart from this lack of unified action. They took the apathy of the West as a sign that they could do as they pleased to the Jews.

Soon after the Evian Conference, violence against the Jews escalated. By November, the Nazis had carried out their giant pogrom of destruction that became known as *Kristallnacht*—crystal night or night of the broken glass.

What Are Your Attitudes?

Have you ever thought about your own attitudes toward people who are different from you? Are you prejudiced at all? Before answering, consider the following questions:

- Have you ever made a negative comment about another person based on race, religion, nationality, or gender?

- Have you ever used an insulting term to describe a person based on race, religion, nationality, or gender?

- Have you ever heard a friend make that kind of negative comment or use that kind of insulting term?

- If so, how did you respond? What did you say? What did you do?

- Have you ever gone along with a hate crime?

- Have you ever known a victim of a hate crime?

- If so, what did you say or do to help?

Being aware of your attitudes is important. Always remember that prejudice can lead to violence.

What Can You Do?

In large and small ways, every person can take a stand against prejudice. Here are some things you could do:

- Never make an insulting comment about another person based on race, religion, nationality, or gender.

- Never use an insulting term to refer to another person of a different race, religion, nationality, or gender.

- If you hear a friend make an insulting comment or use an insulting term of this kind, speak up.

- If you learn of a hate crime, report it. Hate crimes are against the law.

- If you know a victim of a hate crime, give a helping hand.

A Modern Day Protest Against Hate

Today's hate groups are like the Nazis in another way. They too respond to group protest. The town of Billings, Montana, learned this lesson from experience.

On a quiet December evening in 1993, neo-Nazis tossed a cinder block through a window in the home of Tammie and Brian Schnitzer. It sent huge pieces of broken glass into the bedroom of their five-year-old son, Isaac. The Schnitzers are Jewish, and their window was decorated with a menorah. The menorah is a symbol for Chanukah, the Jewish festival of lights.

Fortunately, Isaac was playing with his little sister, Rachel, in another room when his window was broken.

That night Brian Schnitzer put his children in sleeping bags under the big bed in his bedroom.

When Margaret MacDonald read about this incident in the local paper, she called her pastor. Margaret had already been active fighting prejudice in Billings. She had been working to get people from all over town to sign a petition opposing bigotry. Now she asked her pastor to have the children in their Sunday school draw menorahs to put in their windows at home. So did many others. As Becky Thomas explained it, "It's easy to go around saying you support some good cause, but this was different. . . . I told my husband, 'Now we know how the Schnitzers feel.'"[14]

Margaret's idea was accepted and flourished. The police gave their support. The local newspaper published a picture of a menorah for families to put up in their windows. Local businesses also helped by passing out copies of the picture. One business put up a billboard that said "Not in Our Town! No Hate. No Violence. Peace on Earth." People in about six thousand homes displayed menorahs in their windows to support their Jewish neighbors.[15]

The hate groups backed down. The hate crimes stopped. The town of Billings continued its united stand against prejudice. Over two hundred fifty Christians joined their Jewish neighbors for a Passover meal. They organized and attended school meetings to promote racial harmony. They planned combined holiday activities. Many Billings families decided to save their menorahs for the next Chanukah season. Said Brian Schnitzer, "The Chanukah miracle occurred only after people fought for freedom. That happened in ancient times, and it happened in Billings just last year."[16]

Taking a stand against hatred requires courage and determination. But, as the town of Billings discovered, the results can be enormously satisfying. Individuals working together can make a difference.

Standing up for what is fair and remembering the past are two ways of making sure that the Holocaust never happens again. As Peter Gersh, a Holocaust survivor in Poland, put it:

> We who survived believe that there is a meaning to our survival. It places on us a special responsibility to tell what happened. Not only to our children and friends but to the whole world. To never lower the guard. To stand up for the oppressed. To build a world based on justice, peace, and dignity for everyone. That would be the best and a lasting memorial to our parents, brothers, sisters, relatives, and friends that [sic] perished in the Holocaust.[17]

Appendix

Holocaust Museums in North America

Allentown Jewish Archives
Holocaust Resource Center
702 North 22nd Street
Allentown, PA 18104

Anne Frank Center, U.S.A.
584 Broadway, Suite 408
New York, NY 10003

Aushwitz Study Foundation, Inc.
P.O. Box 2232
Huntington Beach, CA 92647

Center for Holocaust Studies
Brookdale Community College
765 Newman Spring Road
Lincroft, NJ 07738

The Dallas Memorial Center for Holocaust Studies
7900 Northhaven Road
Dallas, TX 75230

Dayton Holocaust Resource Center
100 East Woodbury Drive
Dayton, OH 45415

El Paso Holocaust Museum and Study Center
405 Wallenberg Drive
El Paso, TX 79912

Fortunoff Video Archive for Holocaust Testimonies
Sterling Memorial Library
Room 331-C
Yale University
New Haven, CT 06520

Holocaust Awareness Museum
Gratz College
Old York Road & Melrose Avenue
Melrose Park, PA 19126

Holocaust Center of the North Shore Jewish Federation
McCarthy School
70 Lake Street, Room 108
Peabody, MA 01960

The Holocaust Center of Northern California
639 14th Avenue
San Francisco, CA 94118

Holocaust Education and Memorial Centre of Toronto
4600 Bathurst Street
Willowdale, Ontario
Canada M2R 3V2

Holocaust Education Center and Memorial
  Museum of Houston
2425 Fountainview Drive, Suite 270
Houston, TX 77057

Holocaust/Genocide Studies Center
Plainview/Old Bethpage
John F. Kennedy High School
50 Kennedy Drive
Plainview, NY 11803

Holocaust Learning Center
David Posnack Jewish Center
5850 South Pine Island Road
Davie, FL 33328

Holocaust Memorial Foundation of Illinois
4255 West Main Street
Skokie, IL 60076

Holocaust Memorial Resource and Education
Center of Central Florida
851 North Maitland Avenue
Maitland, FL 32751

Holocaust Resource Center
Bureau of Jewish Education
441 East Avenue
Rochester, NY 14607

Holocaust Resource Center
Keene State College
Mason Library
229 Main Street
Keene, NH 03431

Holocaust Resource Center and Archives
Queensborough Community College
222-05 56th Ave.
Bayside, NY 11364

Holocaust Resource Center of Kean College
Thompson Library, Second Floor
Kean College
Union, NJ 07083

Holocaust Resource Center of Minneapolis
8200 West 33rd Street
Minneapolis, MN 55426

Holocaust Studies Center
The Bronx High School of Science
75 West 205th Street
Bronx, NY 10468

Leo Baeck Institute
129 East 73rd Street
New York, NY 10021

**A Living Memorial to the Holocaust—Museum
of Jewish Heritage**
342 Madison Avenue, Suite 706
New York, NY 10173

**Martyrs Memorial and Museum of the Holocaust
of the Jewish Federation Council**
6505 Wilshire Boulevard
Los Angeles, CA 90048

Joseph Meyerhoff Library
Baltimore Hebrew University
5800 Park Heights Avenue
Baltimore, MD 21215

The Montreal Holocaust Memorial Center
5151 Cote Street
Catherine Road
Montreal, Quebec
Canada H3W 1M6

Oregon Holocaust Resource Center
2900 Southwest Peaceful Lane
Portland, OR 97201

Rhode Island Holocaust Memorial Museum
JCC of Rhode Island
401 Elmgrove Avenue
Providence, RI 02906

Rockland Center for Holocaust Studies, Inc.
17 South Madison Avenue
Spring Valley, NY 10977

Simon Wiesenthal Center
9760 West Pico Boulevard
Los Angeles, CA 90035

Sonoma State University Holocaust Center
Alliance for the Study of the Holocaust
Rohnert Park, CA 94928

St. Louis Center for Holocaust Studies
12 Millstone Campus Drive
St. Louis, MO 63146

Tampa Bay Holocaust Memorial Museum and
  Educational Center
5001 113th Street (Duhme Road)
St. Petersburg, FL 33708

United States Holocaust Memorial Museum
100 Raoul Wallenberg Place, Southwest
(15th Street and Independence Avenue)
Washington, DC 20024

The Vanderbilt University Holocaust Art Collection
Vanderbilt University
402 Sarratt Student Center
Nashville, TN 37240

Zachor Holocaust Center
1753 Peachtree Road, Northeast
Atlanta, GA 30309

Chapter Notes

Chapter 1

1. William L. Shirer, *The Rise and Fall of the Third Reich* (New York: Simon & Schuster, 1960) p. 112.

2. Ibid., p. 166.

3. Raul Hilberg, *The Destruction of the European Jews* (Chicago: Quadrangle Books, 1961), p. 3.

4. Shirer, pp. 259, 281–283.

5. United States Holocaust Memorial Museum Archives, Record Group A 203: Eva Edmands Testimony, p. 11.

Chapter 2

1. Raul Hilberg, *The Destruction of the European Jews* (Chicago: Quadrangle Books, 1961), pp. 5–7.

2. Michael Berenbaum, *The World Must Know* (Boston: Little, Brown and Company, 1993), p. 16.

3. Hilberg, pp. 5–7.

4. Ibid., p. 105.

5. Louis Golding, *The Jewish Problem* (England: Penguin Books, 1938), pp. 122–123; William L. Shirer, *The Rise and Fall of the Third Reich* (New York: Simon & Schuster, 1960), pp. 241–244.

6. Lucy S. Dawidowicz, *The War against the Jews 1933–1945* (New York: Seth Press, 1986), pp. 311–339.

7. Berenbaum, p. 54.

8. United States Holocaust Memorial Museum Archives, Record Group 99, Religious Victims, 02: Anna Bluethe Testimony, Folder 1, p. 3.

9. Berenbaum, p. 54.

10. USHMMA, RG-02.099, F1, p. 7.

11. Hilberg, p. 126.

12. Berenbaum, p. 74.

13. United States Holocaust Memorial Museum Archives, Record Group 72, Religious Victims, 02: Joseph Soski Memoirs, Folder 1, p. 30.

14. William W. Mishell, *Kaddish for Kovno: Life and Death in a Lithuanian Ghetto 1941–1945* (Chicago: Chicago Review Press, 1988), p. 99.

15. Hilberg, p. 172.

16. Ibid., pp. 182, 189.

17. Mishell, pp. 93–94.

18. Hilberg, p. 256.

Chapter 3

1. Henry Friedlander, "The Nazi Camps," *Genocide: Critical Issues of the Holocaust* edited by Alex Grobman and Daniel Landes, (Los Angeles and Chappaqua, New York: The Simon Wiesenthal Center and Rossel Books, 1983), p. 222.

2. William L. Shirer, *The Rise and Fall of the Third Reich* (New York: Simon & Schuster, 1960), p. 272.

3. Arno J. Mayer, *Why Did the Heavens Not Darken?* (New York: Pantheon Books, 1988), p. 330.

4. Friedlander, pp. 222–223.

5. Anton Gill, *The Journey Back from Hell: An Oral History—Conversations with Concentration Camp Survivors* (New York: William Morrow & Co., 1988), p. 254.

6. Friedlander, p. 225.

7. United States Holocaust Memorial Museum Archives, Record Group 72, Religious Victims, 02: Joseph Soski: Memories of a Vanished World, Folder 1, © 1991, p. 54.

8. Friedlander, p. 226.

9. Mayer, p. 336.

10. Ibid., pp. 336–337.

11. Benjamin B. Ferencz, *Less Than Slaves* (Cambridge, Mass.: Harvard University Press, 1979), pp. 25–30.

12. Rhoda G. Lewin, editor, *Witness to the Holocaust: An Oral History* (Boston: Twayne Publishers, 1990), p. 46.

13. USHMMA, RG-02.072, F1, p. 55.

14. Lewin, pp. 5–6.

15. Raul Hilberg, *The Destruction of the European Jews* (Chicago: Quadrangle Books, 1961), pp. 216–219.

16. Friedlander, pp. 229–230; Lucy S. Dawidowicz, *The War against the Jews 1933–1945* (New York: Holt, Rinehart & Winston, 1975), p. 135.

17. Deborah Dwork, *Children with a Star: Jewish Youth in Nazi Europe* (New Haven: Yale University Press, 1991), p. xxxiii.

18. Ibid.

19. Editors of Time-Life Books, *The Apparatus of Death* (Alexandria, Va.: Time-Life Books, 1991), pp. 104–110.

20. Lewin, p. 98.

21. Nora Levin, *The Holocaust: The Destruction of European Jewry 1933–1945* (New York: Schocken Books, 1968), p. 312.

22. Leni Yahil, *The Holocaust: The Fate of European Jewry, 1932–1945* (New York: Oxford University Press, 1990), pp. 366–368.

23. Dawidowicz, p. 149.

24. Azriel Eisenberg, *Witness to the Holocaust* (New York: Pilgrim Press, 1981), p. 304.

Chapter 4

1. Editors of Time-Life Books, *The Apparatus of Death* (Alexandria, Va.: Time-Life Books, 1991), p. 82.

2. Ibid., p. 16.

3. William E Shapiro and the Staff of CBS News, *Trial at Nuremberg* (New York: Franklin Watts, 1967), p. 23.

4. Carol Rittner and Sondra Myers, editors, *The Courage to Care: Rescuers of Jews During the Holocaust* (New York: New York University Press, 1986), p. 7.

5. Anton Gill, *The Journey Back from Hell: An Oral History—Conversations with Concentration Camp Survivors* (New York: William Morrow & Co., 1988), p. 29.

6. Editors of Time-Life Books, p. 13.

7. Ina Friedman, *The Other Victims* (Boston: Houghton Mifflin, 1990), p. 64.

8. Lucy S. Dawidowicz, *The War against the Jews 1933–1945* (New York: Holt, Rinehart & Winston, 1975), p. 132.

9. Leni Yahil, *The Holocaust: The Fate of European Jewry, 1932–1945* (New York: Oxford University Press, 1990), p. 309.

10. Dawidowicz, p. 134.

11. Friedman, pp. 7–9.

12. Michael Burleigh and Wolfgang Wipperman, *The Racial State: Germany 1933–1945* (Cambridge, Mass.: Cambridge University Press, 1991), p. 54.; Editors of Time-Life Books, pp. 42–47.

13. Editors of Time-Life Books, p. 83.

14. Friedman, pp. 18–20.

15. Nora Levin, *The Holocaust: The Destruction of European Jewry 1933–1945* (New York: Schocken Books, 1968), p. 668.

16. Barbara Rogasky, *Smoke and Ashes* (New York: Holiday House, 1988), p. 61.

17. Friedman, pp. 47–49.

18. David W. Dunlap, "Personalizing the Nazis' Homosexual Victims," *The New York Times* (June 26, 1995), pp. A1, B4; Gill, pp. 32–34.

19. Dunlap, p. B4.

20. Editors of Time-Life Books, pp. 16, 62, 65, 87.

21. Michael Berenbaum, *The World Must Know* (Boston: Little, Brown and Company, 1993), p. 127.

22. Editors of Time-Life Books, pp. 86–87.

Chapter 5

1. Gay Block and Malka Drucker, *Rescuers, Portraits of Moral Courage in the Holocaust* (New York: Holmes & Meier Publishers, Inc., 1992), p. 175.

2. Leni Yahil, *The Holocaust: The Fate of European Jewry, 1932–1945* (New York: Oxford University Press, 1990), p. 582.

3. Azriel Eisenberg, *Witness to the Holocaust* (New York: The Pilgrim Press, 1981), pp. 379–382.

4. Barbara Rogasky, *Smoke and Ashes* (New York: Holiday House, 1988), p. 148.

5. Ibid., p. 145.

6. Ruud van der Rol and Rian Verhoeven, *Anne Frank: Beyond the Diary* (New York: Viking Press, 1993), pp. 48, 56–57.

7. Ruud van der Rol and Rian Verhoeven, *Anne Frank: Beyond the Diary, A Photographic Remembrance* (New York: Viking, 1993), p. 104.

8. Anne Frank, *Anne Frank: The Diary of a Young Girl* (New York: Picket Books, 1972), p. 237.

9. van der Rol and Verhoeven, pp. 108–109.

10. Carol Rittner and Sondra Myers, editors, *The Courage to Care: Rescuers of Jews During the Holocaust* (New York: New York University Press, 1986), p. 59.

11. Peter Hellman, *Avenue of the Righteous* (New York: Atheneum, 1980), pp. 168–267.

12. Rittner and Myers, p. 42.

13. Ibid., pp. 38–43.

14. Philip P. Hallie, *Lest Innocent Blood Be Shed* (New York: Harper & Row, 1979), p. 120.

15. Ibid., pp. 134–200.

16. Eric Silver, *The Book of the Just: The Unsung Heroes Who Rescued Jews from Hitler* (New York: Grove Press, 1992), p. 19.

17. Rogasky, p. 144.

18. Silver, p. 3.; Lucy S. Dawidowicz, *The War against the Jews, 1933–1945* (New York: Holt, Rinehart & Winston, 1975), pp. 357–401.

19. Yahil, p. 587.

20. Michael Berenbaum, *The World Must Know* (Boston: Little, Brown and Company, 1993), pp. 166–169.

21. Harold Flender, *Rescue in Denmark* (New York: Simon & Schuster, 1963), pp. 252–253.

22. Arnold Geier, *Heroes of the Holocaust* (Miami: Londonbook, 1993), p. 17.

Chapter 6

1. Michael Berenbaum, *The World Must Know* (Boston: Little, Brown and Company, 1993), p. 183.

2. Robert H. Abzug, *Inside the Vicious Heart* (New York: Oxford University Press, 1985), p. 30.

3. Berenbaum, pp. 184.

4. Ibid., pp. 186–189.

5. Abzug, p.31.

6. Ibid., p. 92.

7. Terrence Petty, "Camp of Death: GI Liberators Recall Horror," *The Patriot Ledger,* April 29/30, 1995, p. 6.

8. Abzug, p. 142.

9. Grahem A. Cosmas and Albert E. Cowdrey, *Medical Service in the European Theater of Operations,* Center of Military History, United States Army, Washington, D.C., 1992.

10. Abzug, p. 142.

11. Ibid., p. 147.

12. Ibid., pp. 161–162.

13. William E. Shapiro, editor, and the Staff of CBS News, *Trial at Nuremberg* (New York: Franklin Watts, 1967), p. 1.

14. Robert E. Conot, *Justice at Nuremberg* (New York: Harper & Row, 1983), pp. 9–10; Ann Tusa and John Tusa, *The Nuremberg Trial* (New York: Atheneum, 1984), p. 22.

15. Shapiro, p. 8.

16. Conot, p. 73.

17. Shapiro, p. 48.

18. Tusa and Tusa, pp. 133, 138, 504.

19. Rhoda G. Lewin, editor, *Witness to the Holocaust: An Oral History* (Boston: Twayne Publishers, 1990), p. 76.

20. Andrea Hamilton, "For Some, a Final Christmas Party," *Boston Globe,* December 12, 1994, p. 3.

21. Doreen Carvajal, "Lighting Candles to Keep the Flame of the Holocaust Alive," *The New York Times,* May 1, 1995, p. B2.

Chapter 7

1. AP Report, "Attacks on Jews Rise, Group Says," *Boston Globe,* April 11, 1995, p. 10.

2. Alan Cowell, "Attacks on Austrian Gypsies Deepen Fear of Neo-Nazis," *The New York Times,* February 21, 1995, p. A1.

3. *Criminal Justice Information Services Uniform Crime Reports, Hate Crime–1993,* U.S. Department of Justice, Federal Bureau of Investigation, Criminal Justice Information Services Division.

4. AP Report, April 11, 1995, p. 10.

5. Bartlett, John, *Familiar Quotations* (Boston: Little, Brown and Company, 1968), p. 867.

6. Jonathan Alter, "After the Survivors," *Newsweek,* December 20, 1993, p. 117.

7. David Ansen, "Spielberg's Obsession," *Newsweek,* December 20, 1993, p. 113.

8. Anton Gill, *The Journey Back from Hell: An Oral History—Conversations with Concentration Camp Survivors* (New York: William Morrow & Co., 1988), p. 2.

9. Ansen, p. 113.

10. Carol Rittner and Sondra Myers, editors, *The Courage to Care: Rescuers of Jews During the Holocaust* (New York: New York University Press, 1986), p. 43.

11. Elizabeth Neuffer, "Germans Debate Role of Nation's Past in Its Future," *Boston Globe,* May 7, 1995, p. 23.

12. Ibid., p. 23.

13. Ibid.

14. Claire Safran, "Not in Our Town," *Redbook Magazine,* November 1994, p. 83.

15. Ibid., p. 126.

16. Barbara Sofer, "Not in Our Town," *Woman's Day,* November 22, 1994, p. 40.

17. United States Holocaust Memorial Museum Archives, Record Group 76, Religious Victims, 02: Peter Gersh Testimony, Folder 1, p. 5.

Glossary

Anschluss—Germany's takeover of Austria in March 1938.

Aryans—Blond-haired, blue-eyed members of the so-called "Master Race." In Hitler's mind, they were the only pure Germans.

concentration camp—An area where the Nazis "concentrated" prisoners in one place, treated them brutally, and forced them to work under subhuman conditions.

death camp—An area where the Nazis carried out the mass murder of their captives.

Einsatzgruppen—Mobile Nazi killing units.

Gestapo—The Nazi secret police.

ghetto—A small, rundown area of a town where a specific group of people, such as the Jews under Nazi persecution, are isolated and forced to live.

Kristallnacht—The Nazi pogrom of November 9, 1938. Literally translated it means "Crystal Night" or "Night of Broken Glass." The name comes from all of the glass that was shattered during this violent outburst against the Jews.

Lebensraum—Literally translated it means "living space." This was the name of Hitler's plan to take over Eastern Europe and get rid of all of the Jews, Slavs, and other groups he considered inferior. His goal was to free the area for the Aryans.

Mein Kampf—Literally translated it means "my struggle." It was the title of Hitler's autobiography. He wrote most of it while he was in prison. It details his ideas about how to make Germany a world power.

Munich Agreement—Hitler's September 29, 1939, agreement with England and France that allowed Germany to take over Czechoslovakia without a fight.

Nuremberg Laws—Laws established on September 15, 1935, wiping out the rights of Germany's Jews.

Nuremberg Trials—Post-war trials of Nazi war criminals. The trials were held in Nuremberg, Germany, beginning on October 6, 1945.

pogrom—An organized display of violence and persecution.

S.A.—*Sturmabteilung* or Brown Shirts. They were stormtroopers and early supporters of Hitler who broke up opponents' meetings and hastened Hitler's rise to power.

S.S.—*Schutzstaffel* or Black Shirts. They were the private, powerful, elite Nazi army, responsible for countless atrocities.

Yad Vashem—A memorial in Jerusalem, Israel, in honor of those who died and those who fought to save lives during the Holocaust.

Further Reading

Atkinson, Linda. *In Kindling Flame: The Story of Hannah Senesh, 1921–1944.* New York: Lothrop, Lee & Shepard, 1985.

Berenbaum, Israel. *My Brother's Keeper.* New York: G.P. Putnam's Sons, 1985.

Frank, Anne. . New York: Doubleday & Company, 1989.

Gies, Miep. *Anne Frank Remembered: The Story of the Woman Who Helped to Hide the Frank Family.* New York: Simon & Schuster, 1987.

Koehn, Ilse. *Mischling, Second Degree: My Childhood in Nazi Germany.* New York: Greenwillow Books, 1977.

Laird, Christa. *Shadow of the Wall.* New York: Greenwillow Books, 1990.

Leitner, Isabella. *Fragments of Isabella: A Memoir of Auschwitz.* New York: Thomas Y. Crowell, 1978.

Meltzer, Milton. *Rescue: The Story of how Gentiles Saved Jews in the Holocaust.* New York: Harper and Row, 1988.

Moskin, Marietta. *I am Rosemarie.* New York: John Day, 1972.

Roth-Hano, Renee. *Touch Wood: A Girlhood in Occupied France.* New York: Four Winds Press, 1988.

Schuman, Michael A. *Elie Wiesel: Voice From the Holocaust.* Hillside, N.J.: Enslow Publishers, Inc., 1994.

Siegal, Aranka. *Upon the Head of the Goat: A Childhood in Hungary 1939–1944.* New York: Farrar, Straus & Giroux, 1981.

Volavkova, Hana, editor. *I Never Saw Another Butterfly: Children's Drawings and Poems from Terezin Concentration Camp 1942–1944.* New York: Schocken Books, 1978.

Wiesel, Elie. *Night.* New York: Hill & Wang, 1960.

Young People Speak: Surviving the Holocaust in Hungary. New York: Franklin Watts, 1993.

Index

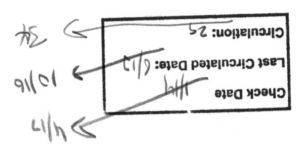

Check Date ___11/16___

Last Circulated Date: 6/17

Circulation: 25

4/17

10/16

3/4